ADVANCE PRAISE FOR
RECHARGE IN MINUTES

"If you've ever wondered where your day went or how you'll face tomorrow's challenges, RECHARGE IN MINUTES will seem like it was written just for you! Simple, insightful, and practical advice."

—Vincent M. Roazzi
Author, *The Spirituality of Success:*
Getting Rich with Integrity

"A recent Wall Street Journal *article explained that the binge/purge method of dealing with stress is not effective. We need to recharge on a daily basis. If you're thinking 'Easier said than done,' read this book. Not one of Zoglio's quick-lift ideas takes more than ten minutes. A great tool for quick renewal."*

—Dr. Alan Elko
Superintendent, West Chester Area School District

"RECHARGE IN MINUTES is the perfect sequel to Create a Life That Tickles Your Soul. *This time the author helps us to enhance each day! The quick-lift method is an effective antidote for fatigue, stress, or lagging motivation. Zoglio is a master at combining practical advice, wisdom, and inspiration into one user-friendly package."*

—Bill Lawton
Smoking Cessation Counselor

"This book is immensely readable, the ideas are powerful, and Zoglio's strategy is wise. If you want to enhance both success and happiness at the same time, try these quick-lift strategies."

—J. Henry Warren
Aerospace Manufacturer, CEO,
Author of *Storm Keeper*

"This book punches the energy dilemma right in the nose! I ordered copies for our entire leadership team, and it will be our soft skills focus for 2003."

—Dan Lambert
Plant General Manager, American Electric Power

A GREAT LIFE IS BORN IN THE SOUL,
GROWN IN THE MIND,
AND LIVED FROM THE HEART.

From *Create a Life That Tickles Your Soul*

RECHARGE IN MINUTES

THE
QUICK-LIFT WAY
TO LESS STRESS,
MORE SUCCESS,
AND RENEWED
ENERGY!

SUZANNE Willis ZOGLIO, Ph.D.

TOWER HILL  PRESS

Doylestown, Pennsylvania 18901

Published by Tower Hill Press, Doylestown, PA 18901

Printed in the United States of America

Jacket and Interior Design by Dunn+Associates

Library of Congress Cataloging-in-Publication Data

Zoglio, Suzanne
Recharge in minutes: the quick-lift way to less stress,
more success, and renewed energy! / by Suzanne Willis Zoglio. –1st ed.
    p. cm.
Includes bibliographical references and index.
ISBN 0-941668-14-2 (alk. paper)

1. Self-help techniques. 2. Success – Psychological aspects. I. Title.
BF632.Z64 2003
158.1 – dc21
2003007683

*To my readers, clients, and workshop participants
who have generously shared their dreams, stresses,
and recharging successes, thereby co-creating this work.*

TABLE OF CONTENTS

RECHARGE IN MINUTES

The Quick-Lift Way to Less Stress, More Success, and Renewed Energy!

INTRODUCTION

"I'd love to make some changes at work and in my life, but I just can't get myself going." "There are lots of things I want to do, but by the time I finish all I have to do, I'm too tired to do what I want." These are common complaints that I hear from workshop participants, coaching clients, and even family and friends. Living and working in our fast-paced society often means that by the time we've finished our day's work or caregiving, we're too tired to gear up for other things that are important to a satisfying life. We may want to take a painting class, read a good book, or join a gym, but the motivation is hard to find. We may know that our lives would be richer if we'd change jobs, end tumultuous relationships, or take better care of ourselves, but we simply don't have the spunk to pull off such a shift. Our heads say, "Go," but our feet say, "No."

When I wrote *Create a Life That Tickles Your Soul*, I hoped that it would inspire people to live more of the life they really wanted. So it was very gratifying to hear that the book helped readers to gain clarity, confidence, and inspiration. People wrote that the activities helped them to identify what was really important and deal with personal beliefs and habits that were keeping them from living a satisfying life. They also wrote about a strengthened desire to live from the inside out, and a strengthened belief that they could actually create more peace, passion, and purpose in their lives.

It wasn't long, however, before the people who had gained awareness and mapped out a different life plan were inquiring about how to get going—or how to keep going when the going got tough. "How do I find the motivation to change ingrained habits and beliefs, when most days I'm so worn out I just want to flop?" was a common question. Another was: "Now that I know where I want to go, how do I stay charged over time?" It seems the biggest block to living as we wish is a chronic lack of energy.

How did we get into this state—too tired to engage in activities that would add joy and meaning to our lives? It's true that fate sometimes serves up a major energy drain such as divorce, loss, or a serious illness, but most of the time our lack of zest is far less dramatic. Over time, we inadvertently slip into beliefs and habits that rob us of clarity, resilience, and motivation. Soon we are working 24/7, ignoring a need to refuel or doing so only once a year on vacation. We wistfully talk of the days when we will have more time for ourselves—to stretch and relax and maybe give something back. So while we're waiting for someday, we ignore recharging on a daily basis. When there is no daily ebb and flow, we lose our balance. It's a simple accounting matter. If you expend more energy than you take in every day, you'll soon find yourself running on "empty."

So, what are we to do? Certainly, there are many books that offer the secrets to transforming one's life. In fact, I wrote one of them: *Create a Life That Tickles Your Soul*. But, before we can change our *lives* in any substantial way, we have to change how we function each *day*. We have to manage our energy as we would any other precious resource—addressing how we generate it, how we spend it, and how we can conserve it. Over the last three years, I addressed that issue with a column in my online newsletter. The intent of "10 Ideas for Expanding Your Life" was to provide simple, yet powerful ways to expand positive energy immediately. I truly believe that by taking a few minutes every day to refuel, we not only become more effective at coping with life's daily stresses, but also at building a reserve so we have what it takes to move our careers and lives forward.

The response to my newsletter "energizers" was quite astounding. At first, people couldn't believe that a brief activity of only five to ten minutes could pay such big dividends, but renewed zip and an unstoppable attitude were proof enough. Clients, subscribers, and workshop participants reported new levels of energy, optimism, and motivation. I believe many of these quick-lift ideas will work for you too. Give yourself a little energy boost each day and you'll find the power you need to pursue even your biggest dreams.

You may be curious about how these quick-lift activities can be so effective. It is no secret that if we want high energy, we need to take care of ourselves physically—with nutrition, rest, and exercise. Like automobiles, our bodies need such fuel to function effectively. But did you also know that a good portion of our energy is actually *emotional energy?* You might feel as energized after a visit with a dear friend as you do after a good night's sleep. Conversely, you might feel more depleted after a spat with a spouse or being passed over for a promotion, than if you cleaned every room in the house or worked overtime all week. To better understand how emotions affect our energy, think back to a time when you heard a loud noise, had a bad dream, or were publicly embarrassed. Can you remember how your body responded? Emotions such as fear, anger, guilt, or regret increase blood pressure, heart rate, perspiration, and adrenaline production as they trigger what is known as the fight/flight or stress response researched extensively by Dr. Herbert Benson, author of *The Relaxation Response*. Often, after such an event, we feel drained. If the stress response goes unchecked, it negatively affects our health. On the other hand, many mind/body experts (Benson in *Timeless Healing*, Tara Bennett-Goleman in *Emotional Alchemy*, Deepak Chopra in *Ageless Body/Timeless Mind*, Bernie Siegel in *Peace, Love, and Healing)* have shown us how certain beliefs, emotions, and behaviors actually increase positive energy and accelerate healing. Advances in neuroscience confirm what sports psychologists and successful coaches have been proposing for years: different physiological responses are produced when different parts of the brain are activated by thoughts or emotions. The importance of positive emotions to motivation, success, happiness and health has been illuminated by the work of Daniel Goleman (*Emotional Intelligence, Primal Leadership, Destructive Emotions)*. It is safe to say that our minds, bodies, and spirit are very much connected. So while it is certainly prudent to manage our diet and exercise, we should not neglect another important factor that adds zest to life: the management of our emotional energy.

Every day we face situations that can drain us emotionally, lowering our motivation and inspiration. Calling upon my work with clients over the past twenty years, I have focused *Recharge in Minutes* on ten common low-energy states—from mental overload to mind-numbing boredom; from bouts of self-doubt to fear of moving forward; from being annoyed with people to being hungry for connection—and ten ways to reverse each one. In all, you'll find 101 quick-lift ideas on how to shift gears and recharge your inner energy fast! Each "power break" only takes five to ten minutes, so you won't have to turn your life upside down to find more zip. Just stop every now and then to consciously shift your energy from outbound to in. Use these boosters when you sense your energy is getting low, or make them part of your daily routine. In just minutes a day, you'll restore your sense of balance and feel more in charge of your life. With these ideas at your fingertips, you'll build up a can-do attitude that makes you virtually unstoppable. When an energy drain is thrown at you, you'll be able to catch it, shift it, and feel your personal power rise. No matter what low-energy state you slip into, you'll be able to lift yourself out of it quickly. It's true that these quick-lifts will not change your *life*. But they will perk up your *day*. You'll see a difference in your outlook and energy immediately, and the cumulative effect will be even greater. No more collapsing at the end of the day, or wracking your brain for creative ideas. No more overreacting from frazzled nerves, or overcommitting from blurred vision of what's important. No more second-guessing your ability to make the changes you want, or getting stuck in disappointment at your streak of bad luck. In the amount of time you'd spend getting a cup of coffee, you can boost your present energy and—in time—lift your life. Of course, every idea offered won't appeal to you personally—each of us is unique. Try the ideas that you find most appealing. Perhaps some will inspire quick-lift ideas of your own. If so, I'd love to hear from you—and perhaps include some of your ideas in *Recharge in Minutes, Volume 2.*

If you read *Recharge in Minutes* all the way through once, you'll strengthen your resilience overall and build a whole toolbox of energizers to apply as you face everyday challenges. Another option is to use *Recharge in Minutes* as an energy first-aid kit, going straight to the chapter that seems to match whatever low-energy state you are experiencing right now.

In **Chapter One**, you'll find ideas to clear your head when you can't think straight. Perhaps you simply have too much on your mind or too much on your plate. You might feel like a gerbil, frantically running on an exercise wheel, but going nowhere fast. Maybe your mind is racing, you can't sleep, or things keep falling through the cracks. If you're fighting fires much of the time, the quick-lift ideas in this chapter will help you to *focus.*

Turn to **Chapter Two** when you need a vacation, you need it bad, and you need it now. You may be suffering from the all-work-no-play virus that is so prevalent in our 24/7, busy-is-better environment. It's not so much that your mind is muddled, but that you are experiencing battle fatigue. You may not be getting enough rest, enough pampering, or enough fun. The quick-lift ideas in this chapter are all about *chilling out.*

Chapter Three is filled with the right stuff to get you out of a rut. When your energy slumps because you've stayed in your comfort zone too long, the only way out is through the unknown. To feel alive, you've got to shake things up, stretch, and grow. This is not the time to get trapped in "same-old," even if your "same-old" has been pretty good. The quick-lift ideas in this chapter are meant to *rev you up.*

Chapter Four provides ideas on what to do when it's time for antacid. Look here when something's got you all worked up. Things went wrong, you're really worried, or someone's got your blood boiling. The quick-lift ideas presented in this chapter are about *calming down*.

Chapter Five is where to look when you are searching for a great idea, but keep coming up empty-handed. Maybe you have one hour to decide on a great birthday surprise, or a week to complete a cost-cutting plan. Perhaps you're writing a speech and need a powerful close, or are trying to launch your new business on a limited budget. The quick-lift ideas in this chapter show you how to *invite inspiration* in minutes.

In **Chapter Six** the theme is on living a meaningful life. Maybe you've been following other people's rules, and are afraid that in the end you'll regret not following your heart. You might be wondering, "Is this all there is?" Perhaps you have a sinking feeling that life is passing you by, or that you won't leave any legacy behind. The quick-lift ideas in this chapter emphasize *creating meaning* on a daily basis.

Chapter Seven is about finding energy through relationships and dealing with the low energy that comes with a sense of disconnection. If you're feeling as though you're all alone and formerly close bonds are now threadbare or missing, this is where to look. The quick-lift ideas in this chapter will help you to *build (or rebuild) your connections*.

Chapter Eight will seem like an oasis if your self-esteem has shriveled a bit. Perhaps you've experienced a setback, been rejected in some way, or let a great opportunity go by. Maybe you have an inner critic that works overtime or a paranoid side that seems to take everything personally lately. The quick-lift ideas in this chapter are about *boosting confidence*.

Chapter Nine is for when you face a desirable, but unsettling, unknown. Perhaps you are presented with a new job opportunity or a chance to make a difference with your gifts. The prospects may frighten you. "What if it doesn't work out?" you might think. "What if it's a disaster?" "What if getting married, having a baby, starting a business, speaking out, or even keeping quiet doesn't work out?" The quick-lift ideas in this chapter can be used whenever you need to *discover more courage.*

The final chapter of *Recharge in Minutes,* **Chapter Ten,** is for the times when you just can't seem to catch a break. Maybe you lose your job—and then someone smashes into your car. Or you get chewed out, lose your wallet, and find a leak in the roof—all in the same week. Whatever dark cloud seems to be hovering over you, here is where to turn. The quick-lift ideas in this chapter are about *acknowledging abundance*—when it seems to be sadly missing.

So, begin at the beginning if you'd like to rev up your life in general, or pick out a chapter that seems to match your situation at present. Whichever approach you choose, it is my sincerest wish that you find these quick-lift ideas useful and this book a helpful tool for revving up your energy and moving your life forward. Here's to living true, living large, and remembering to recharge!

I CAN'T THINK STRAIGHT!

**FINDING
FOCUS**

Chapter 1

I CAN'T THINK STRAIGHT!

Your mind is racing at a breakneck speed—changing direction every few seconds. Perhaps you are plagued by phones ringing, kids demanding attention, customer complaints, employee tiffs, or simply too much on your plate. Whatever your situation, it's as though you need a traffic controller for your brain. One thought takes off. Another crosses into the same path. Several others circle in a holding pattern, waiting for permission to land. If only you could close your thought-port—just for a few moments. It would give you time to sort things out and see more clearly what is most important. You'd feel more in sync from the inside out.

You can calm mental fireworks by practicing techniques that help you to turn down the noise, hear your inner voice, release past concerns, and focus on your priorities. Whether you "shut down" for one minute or ten, you'll notice the difference. Try two short breaks throughout the day, or take one longer break. It's up to you. Whatever time you can spare will add to your clarity.

Just don't fall into the trap of postponing your refocusing break until you have more time. No matter how rich or poor, how wise or uninformed, we all have the same twenty-four hours each day. It's how we choose to use that time that makes the difference. You can race from activity to activity without taking a breath, or you can choose to stop all incoming mind traffic long enough to assess what is best for you next. Imagine what a few minutes of centering might do for you. Lift your mood? Improve productivity? Enhance your creativity? Boost your confidence?

When you can't think straight, it's time to reset your inner compass. Here are ten quick-lifts to help fine-tune your focus. Some take as little as two minutes; none take more than ten. A small investment for clearer direction, don't you think?

Working with a mind in overdrive is like playing darts blindfolded: a bull's-eye is unlikely and mistakes can be painful.

—Suzanne Zoglio

TEN WAYS TO FIND FOCUS FAST!

These quick-lifts will help slow your brain traffic to a normal pace, making you more effective in directing your energy. Read over all ten and then pick one that appeals to you. In just a few minutes you'll feel less scattered, more focused, and full of energy.

1 **Practice "Morning Intent"**

2 **Do, Defer, or Delegate**

3 **Learn to *Really* Breathe**

4 **Complete One Thing**

5 **Throw One Back**

6 **Get Physical**

7 **Accept a Helping Hand**

8 **Get Rid of the Ghosts**

9 **Stop Shoulding on Yourself**

10 **Plan Tomorrow Today**

Quick-Lift 1
PRACTICE "MORNING INTENT"

How often do you start each day by hitting the bricks running? *Before your feet even touch the floor, you're probably reviewing your have-to list: what you have to pick up, whom you have to call, which projects you have to complete. If that's your normal routine, your day is likely to be busy, but not necessarily on target with your priorities. Thinking of all you have to do is not the same as making room for what is really important to you. To sharpen your focus, begin each day by planning from the inside out —using a practice I call "morning intent."*

- Each morning, before you get out of bed, while you shower, travel to work, or land at your desk, set your compass for the day by answering these questions:

  What kind of person do I want to be today?

  What two to three things do I want to **accomplish** today? *Note: The operative word here is "want," not "should."*

  Where can I make a difference in someone's life?

If you start each day briefly focusing on what is meaningful to you, your personal values will shape your choices all day, helping you to stay grounded when your mind threatens to carry you away. You will feel more in control and less likely to get caught up in just putting out fires.

Quick-Lift 2
DO, DEFER, OR DELEGATE

When your brain screams, "Hurry up. You're not doing enough," it's time to stop and prioritize. This three-minute planning break will put you back in the driver's seat. Instead of reacting to every "fire," you'll finish what's important first. With less on your plate, you'll be able to concentrate.

- Write down the top ten things you'd like to complete today.

- Rate each item 1, 2, or 3 (1 = must-do today; 2 = must-do, not necessarily today; and 3 = doesn't necessarily need to be done by you at all).

- Now, "actionize" by priorities (1 = do, 2 = defer, 3 = delegate or dump).

For a quick-lift, try this prioritizing break right now, and then again later in the day. See if your priorities change throughout the day. To maintain focus every day, consider making the 3Ds a habit!

15

Quick-Lift 3
LEARN TO *REALLY* BREATHE

When you are hassled, your breathing becomes shallow and your brain is deprived of much-needed oxygen. No wonder you can't think! Try this cleansing breath technique.

- Close your door or go to a quiet place. Sit in a comfortable chair with your feet flat and your spine straight. Close your eyes and place your hand just above your waist. Now inhale slowly —to the count of six—and feel the air inflate your rib cage, as if it were a balloon pushing against your hand. Relax your chest or lower your shoulders.

- Hold for two seconds in the inflated state. Now, slowly exhale to the count of six, letting your "balloon" empty slowly and your hand sink closer to your spine. Let any tension in your neck and shoulders melt away. Say, "ahhhhh" silently, or "God," "peace," or "yes."

- Repeat for a total of eight deep breaths (in two to four minutes).

When your mind is in overdrive, take a breather—literally!

Quick-Lift 4
COMPLETE ONE THING

When *we can't think straight, it's often because we have too much stuff on our plates. Decisions deferred or actions delayed don't go away; they just add to your pile. One way out of this clutter is to complete things systematically, before starting something new. Decide, act, complete.*

- Make or review your to-do list for the week —or the day—or the hour.

- Now pick one item that you can complete or one decision you can make in five minutes or less. Make a phone call? Send an email? Decide what to have for lunch? Order a birthday bouquet? Jog in place?

- Great! Now cross it off your list and say out loud: "Done!" No matter how small a task, give yourself credit for completing it. As your list shrinks, your sense of control and competence expands. One success sets you up for another.

As you become a master of completion, you will be spurred on by your obvious progress. Feel your head clear as you cross one more thing off your list. Every time you complete something, you reduce the number of things you have to remember to do. When your mind has fewer incompletes to keep track of, it won't need to keep switching tracks.

17

Quick-Lift 5
THROW ONE BACK

When your mind is racing, it is often because you have caught too many little fish while you were casting for the big ones. It's up to you to know when to say "no" and throw the little ones back.

- What's one "little fish" you recently picked up from a boss, subordinate, friend, or family member? Maybe you're already wishing you hadn't said, "yes." It might be going to take more time than you originally thought. The circumstances may have changed since you signed on.

- Okay, here's where the rubber meets the road. Contact that person who lured you into a "little fish" commitment and give it back. Of course it's hard—none of us wants to risk disappointing someone—but bite the bullet. Pick up the phone or walk down the hall and tell the person that it is not possible for you to help out after all.

If you start to feel embarrassed, don't! You are righting a situation that was wrong in the first place. Okay, you made a mistake. Any discomfort you feel will be offset by the relief of clearing one thing off your plate. Next time you'll think before you get hooked. Maybe you'll even learn to say "no" more often or at least not volunteer when you have a full plate.

Quick-Lift 6
GET PHYSICAL

When our minds race so rapidly that we don't know which way is "up," it often helps to get physical. It may seem ironic, but it works. As you focus your energy on a physical task, the "traffic" in your mind will begin to thin out.

- Go for a walk.

- Run up and down a set of stairs, or hit the treadmill, if you have one handy.

- Dig in the garden, play with the dog, or wash a floor.

- Wherever you are, stop for three minutes of push-ups, sit-ups, or jumping jacks.

- At work, shoot a few baskets (into the wastebasket) or sprint down to the corner café to pick up that latte or lunch.

If the energy drain is all in your head, get the lead out, and move the rest of you. It's astounding how much mental clarity you can bring about by getting your body involved. See if you don't feel more self-directed after shifting your energy from your head to your feet.

Quick-Lift 7
ACCEPT A HELPING HAND

When we really need a break, it's often because we are trying to do everything alone. We might not know what we want, hesitate to ask for help, or hint rather than ask for the kind of help we'd like. Also, we may be too critical about how someone helps. In the interest of your mental and physical health, try a more effective way to getting the help you deserve.

- The first step to getting what you want is to know what that is. What do you truly need today? Could your spouse take over a task at home? Would a coworker represent you at a meeting? Might a friend meet you for lunch? Could you use a miracle?

- The second step is admitting that you need help to yourself and then to someone else. The jig is up. You are not a superhero. You need some help.

- Now ask specifically for what would help you most. No hinting or implying. Be assertive. Whether you're asking for divine guidance or help from a mere mortal be clear about what you'd really like.

Remember, if an offer of help does arrive, don't insist that it be done precisely your way. Try not to second-guess or nitpick. You've caught a break—and you deserve it. Now give the "helper" a break. Be grateful.

Quick-Lift 8
GET RID OF THE GHOSTS

One common challenge to managing mind traffic is keeping ghosts of the past at bay. No matter how hard we try to stay in the moment, our attention often wanders back to the past. For clearer thinking, you've got to become a ghostbuster.

- Jot down on the top of a card: "I wonder why ...[somebody did something]." List as many possible answers as you can in sixty seconds. Finish with a "letting go" statement, such as "Whatever the reason, it's done—time to move on." Rip up the card, and if the thought returns, try repeating your letting go statement.

- On another card write: "I wish I'd said...[the brilliant response you thought of later]." Now, either follow up on the earlier interaction with your new response, or save the new comment for a future interaction.

- On a third card, write: "In hindsight, I didn't make the best choice when I decided to [whatever behavior you now regret]." Write as many regrets as surface in sixty seconds. Review your list, and shift your attention to decisions you now face. If your mind wanders back, try repeating something like: "That was then; this is now. I've got bigger fish to fry." Then bring your focus back to the present.

Carrying around thoughts of the past is a problem of sheer volume. Clean out your mind clutter so you can see what's best for you next.

Quick-Lift 9
STOP SHOULDING ON YOURSELF

When you can't think straight, "should" is a good word to eliminate from your vocabulary. It resonates with judgment and guilt, and is often followed by a knee-jerk reaction rather than a deliberate decision. First, post this reminder on your telephone or daily calendar: "There are no shoulds." Then try this quick-lift.

- Check your to-do list for any "shoulds." If you find any, ask a few questions: Am I doing this to avoid conflict? To look good? Out of guilt? Because I want to?

- If you answer, "Because I want to," why are you perceiving it as a "should"? Reframe how you think about it, making it a choice. "I want to" energizes; "I have to" depletes.

- If you *can't* say, "Because I want to," don't do it! Risk displeasing someone, ignore your ego, or find another way to deal with any guilt.

"Shoulding" indicates you have surrendered your power of choice and are following someone else's rules. The next time you find yourself thinking, "I should," ask yourself, "Who says?" The answer may surprise you.

Quick-Lift 10

PLAN TOMORROW TODAY

When *you can't think straight it's so important to plan before you move into action. That way, you won't make hasty decisions or let others pull you off course. The irony is that when we're feeling frazzled is precisely the time when we avoid planning because we haven't the time. One way to increase your sense of control and add a little order to your day is to make a habit of planning your tomorrow at the end of today.*

- At the end of today, review all that you have accomplished. Then write out your plan for tomorrow: what has to be done, when, and about how long each project will take. In what order should you tackle each project? When will you schedule in a quick renewal break? Any pre-appointments you need to work in? Don't forget to schedule in some "emergency response" time. If you're like most of us, you'll need it.

After ten minutes of planning, you should be able to release your fixation on tomorrow's tasks and focus on enjoying your evening. When tomorrow does come, you'll come out of the gate with direction and energy. You'll know where to start and have a plan for getting important things done.

Chapter 2

OH, FOR A WEEK AT THE BEACH!

CHILLING OUT

Chapter 2

OH, FOR A WEEK AT THE BEACH!

What good is success if you're too exhausted to enjoy the prize? Whether you're feeling overworked, underappreciated, or just plain exhausted, the remedy seems clear: a vacation! But what if your vacation is not scheduled for another six months? You need it now. You need it bad. It's so important to curb the energy drain before your fuel gauge registers "empty." Don't wait for your official vacation. Instead, take a mini-vacation—a "refueling" break. Kick back, put your feet up, and relax—even if only for a few minutes. Okay, that's *not* the same as a week at the beach, but it'll keep you from burning out completely or from being too exhausted to move when you finally do take time off.

The problem with our 24/7 society is that most of us think in either/or terms. We think "weekday" or "vacation day," keeping everything about them distinct. On vacation days we dress differently, act differently, eat differently, and use our time differently. We relax, rest, and play. In doing so, we shed some weight, lighten up, laugh and smile more. But then comes Monday, and we leave all of the relaxing behind, not to be seen again until the following weekend—or worse—our next vacation. Sure, we need to schedule our vacations, but we all can take unscheduled vacation-like breaks.

Imagine what your life would be like if you never felt bone-tired again. Suppose you never had to drag yourself through another day, collapsing into the nearest chair, too tired to hug your kids, take the dog for a walk, or even talk on the phone with a friend. Suppose instead, you installed a low-energy detector, and every time it went off, you stopped and gave your battery a charge. That would put you in the driver's seat, wouldn't it? See if any of these quick-lifts restore your energy.

Burn the candle at both ends,
and you can't tell which end is up.

—Suzanne Zoglio

TEN WAYS TO CHILL OUT IN PLACE!

These quick-lifts will help you to refuel when you need a vacation but can't get away. None will be as refreshing as a week at the beach, but each is a sure-fire antidote to that totally exhausted, I-need-it-bad state. Read over all ten and then pick one that appeals to you. In just a few minutes you'll feel less stressed and more alive. Don't be surprised if you start humming a Jimmy Buffet tune.

11 Take a Power Nap

12 Indulge Yourself

13 Wash Away the Stress

14 Unplug from Civilization

15 Engage in Vacation Play

16 Let Someone Pamper You

17 Stand on Your Head

18 Beware the Energy Sappers

19 Conduct a "Feeling" Audit

20 Laugh, Laugh, and Then...Laugh Again

Quick-Lift 11
TAKE A POWER NAP

When *your eyelids feel heavy, your shoulders are drooping, or you find yourself yawning in the middle of a telephone call, it's time to surrender!*

- Lock your door, take the phone off the hook, set your watch (or computer alarm) for ten minutes, and let your next task wait.

- Put your head down on your desk (like in kindergarten), sit in a chair with your feet propped up, stretch out on a rug, or curl up on a sofa (if you're lucky enough to have one nearby).

- Close your eyes, take a few deep, slow breaths, and rest—just as if you were out in a hammock on a Sunday afternoon, taking a good old-fashioned, lazy-days-of-summer nap.

You'll be amazed at how refreshed you'll feel after just ten minutes of shut-eye. So what if you get caught? Just say you're taking a power nap. Hey, if it worked for Edison and Einstein, it just might refresh your inner genius too!

Quick-Lift 12
INDULGE YOURSELF

Think *about a treat that you haven't had in a while —one so delicious that just thinking about it makes you smile. Today, don't settle for any substitutes or next-best things. Take a vacation from all things practical, and go find exactly what you want.*

- It might be a childhood treat that you once adored. Maybe it's a special combination—like Oreo cookies dipped in a tall glass of milk or apple pie with a wedge of cheddar cheese. (My mother used to say, "Apple pie without cheese is like a kiss without a squeeze." While I no longer live in New England, that treat combination is like a mini-vacation for me.)

- What makes your mouth water? Rich Belgian chocolate? Wickedly robust coffee? Walk the extra block for the ice cream flavor that you *really* want.

- Instead of drinking water from that week-old plastic bottle, find a goblet and a slice of lemon.

Forget the food police, and lick your fingers if you want to!

Quick-Lift 13

WASH AWAY THE STRESS

W*hat better way to escape for a quick respite than to find some water? It can be soothing, sensual, quiet, or stimulating. Whether you bathe in it, play in it, listen to it, or drink it, water can be very therapeutic.*

- If you are near a gym, search for a massage showerhead or a whirlpool.

- If it's warm outside and happens to be raining, take a walk, lifting your face to the natural shower.

- If you're lucky enough to have a friend who has an outdoor shower or Jacuzzi, schedule a time to use it.

- Sit by an outdoor fountain or bring a small desktop variety to work.

- If you're near the ocean, stop to listen; if not, listen to a tape of the ocean waves.

It really doesn't matter what water is available to you —water in any form can be very refreshing. As you indulge your senses, imagine the water washing away any stressors —toxic people, toxic thoughts, toxic fears.

Quick-Lift 14

UNPLUG FROM CIVILIZATION

There are times when we'd all like to become hermits and shut out the world. The solitary, Thoreau-like life has its appeal—especially after a morning of back-to-back meetings or chauffeuring a half-dozen ten-year-olds. Well, if you can't make it to Walden Pond just yet, here's a mini-escape that might restore you in place.

- Put a "Do Not Disturb" sign on your door. Turn on your voicemail or answering machine or—if you don't have either—take your telephone off the hook. Turn off any distractions: television, radio, stereo system, cell phone, computer, pager, and all of the lights.

- Light a pine-scented candle, if you can (or close your eyes and imagine the smell of a wood-burning fire).

- In your mind's ear, hear the rain on an old tin roof—or perhaps the haunting song of a barn owl. Listen to the wind as it rustles the leaves—and breathe. For a few moments, enjoy your "cabin in the woods."

If you're not adept at visualization, try listening to Shakti Gawain's Creative Visualization *audiotape, which will guide you through the process. Or, instead of visualizing to unplug from civilization, use the quiet time for silent prayer or meditation. All three methods can bring about relaxation.*

Quick-Lift 15

ENGAGE IN VACATION PLAY

One of the problems with all-or-nothing thinking is that it encourages us to associate certain activities exclusively with weekends or vacations. So, we put off enjoying activities that we could easily enjoy on a normal day. True, you can't scuba dive in your back yard or go deep-sea fishing from your office window, but there are many vacation-type activities that might relax you.

- Read one chapter of a beach novel, or do part of a crossword puzzle.

- Practice your putting or ask the office "pro" for a few pointers.

- Take time out for a conversation at the coffee bar. Share a few jokes.

- Linger over the newspaper, as if you had nowhere to go.

- Build sand castle art without sand: a tinker toy tower or a paperclip sculpture?

- Write a few pages in a journal, just recording whatever thoughts pop into your mind.

If you spend ten minutes a day "playing," by the end of the year you will have vacationed a total of sixty-one hours —more than one full work week!

Quick-Lift 16
LET SOMEONE PAMPER YOU

One *indulgence most of us enjoy on vacation is being served. Whether it's the fresh towels each day, a cold drink by the pool, or just having the paper delivered with morning coffee, pampering certainly reverses any feelings of being overburdened. So for a quick-lift when you're not on vacation, consider letting someone pamper you.*

- If your budget allows, get a quick chair massage during your lunch hour.

- At day's end, ask your significant other to rub your feet or fix you a cup of tea.

- If a coworker offers to bring you back coffee, gratefully accept.

- Find a one-time "hire" to wash your car or windows.

- When a friend offers to treat you to lunch, receive the gift graciously.

- If your boss says you deserve the afternoon off, take it.

- If a neighbor offers to mow your lawn when he does his own, take him up on it.

For those of you who are thinking, "Right! Like anyone would offer to wait on me!" I can only say that if you ask for what you want and believe that you will receive it, you usually do.

Quick-Lift 17
STAND ON YOUR HEAD

Many people find yoga to be very rejuvenating. It not only provides a physical rest (some say it's better than a nap), but it also quiets the mind and soothes the spirit with its emphasis on deep breathing and mindfulness.

- Before you've mastered this ancient relaxing practice, try this yoga-like exercise. Lie on the floor, with your legs elevated (against a wall, your desk, or on a chair) to reverse the blood flow and stretch out your spine.

- If you know basic yoga positions, you can choose the most appropriate to stretch out whatever areas feel constricted, and to increase blood flow to various areas of the body. For instance, the shoulder stand, headstand, or plough can be used quite effectively to fight fatigue in minutes, especially if you've been at a desk or computer all morning.

If you'd like to learn more about yoga, consider taking a basic class at your local YMCA or fitness center, or pick up a videotape at the library. There are many forms of yoga, and you'll surely find one that suits you. Then, you can use it to take a quick rejuvenating break whenever you need one.

Quick-Lift 18
BEWARE THE ENERGY SAPPERS

Have you ever noticed how certain people affect your energy level? You can be with some people for only ten seconds and feel their spark igniting something inside you. On the other hand, there are people who can suck the life out of you in seconds.

- To decrease contact with energy sappers, you need to know who they are before you run into them. Then, even if you can't avoid them, at least you can limit your involvement. Identify three energy sappers in your life. Think about what you can do the next time you meet to avoid getting sucked into a whirlpool of negativity. For example, you could just silently wish the person well, and move on. Or you could limit the time you spend in the vicinity.

- To increase contact with people who radiate positive energy, look for people who always seem to be learning something new, meeting neat people, getting involved in "hot" projects, and generally living life fully. One clue will be how good you feel when you're around them. Pick out one of these people right now, and go borrow some energy.

The best way to deflect negative energy from anger, jealousy, gossip, or fear is to think high-energy thoughts yourself—of peace, generosity, integrity, and love.

Quick-Lift 19
CONDUCT A "FEELING" AUDIT

Often *we feel stressed not because of what we do, but rather how we feel about what we do. Since feelings are powerful motivators, if you increase your awareness of what makes you feel good, you're likely to behave that way more often.*

- Try to remember when, in the last week, you felt "psyched," "pumped," "happy," or "energized." Or, on the other hand, when did you feel "bored," "tired," "over the hill," or "not needed?"

- What contributed to any "low" feelings? For example, did you make a mistake or tell a half-truth? Spend time on something you later felt was a waste? Deny yourself time for something you love, or turn down a chance to learn something new?

- What contributed to any natural highs? For example, did you complete something, meet a challenge, or create something new? Connect with someone in a special way? Engage in something you love? Were you involved in something really important? Able to be of service? Use a unique talent or skill?

In our busy lives, it is easy to push feelings aside. But one way to increase your energy is to enhance your emotional awareness.

Quick-Lift 20
LAUGH, LAUGH, AND THEN...LAUGH AGAIN

What better mini-escape when you're feeling weary, than that of a belly laugh? When relaxed, we laugh more—and that laughter helps us to relax even further—which prompts us to laugh more. You get the picture. Stop! Drop what you're doing, and for no less than three minutes go have some fun—in any way that appeals to you.

• Tell a joke or ask someone else to tell *you* one.

• Read today's comics, buy someone a Dilbert card, or flip through your Calvin & Hobbes calendar until you experience a true belly laugh.

• Not working? Imagine your cat walking around the house under your son's cowboy hat—and the elderly babysitter thinking the hat is possessed. Remember the time you led the entire school assembly in the Pledge of Allegiance—the whole time with your zipper down—or something equally mortifying?

• Can you visualize yourself lip-syncing and gyrating your way through an Elvis tune—in your underwear? Come on, you have to laugh!

It's impossible to laugh and feel burdened at the same time. An active funny bone gives you strength.

Chapter 3

I'M OK...JUST STUCK IN A RUT!

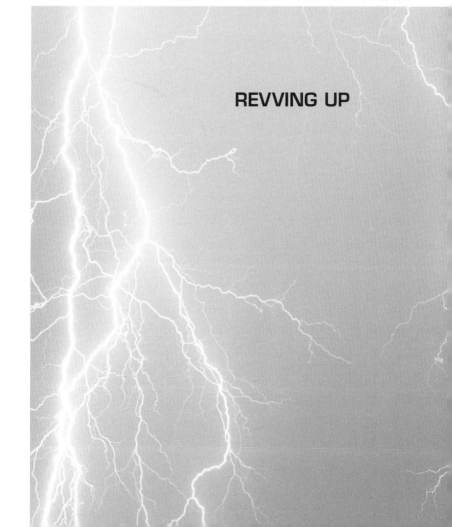

REVVING UP

Chapter 3

I'M OK...JUST STUCK IN A RUT!

Have you ever felt tired, worn out, or a little too old for your years—whatever your age? If so, it might have nothing to do with the number of candles on your birthday cake. Instead, it could be that you've just gotten a bit too settled, allowing your life to go stale.

In physics the principle of entropy explains the natural tendency of all living things to either grow or break down. It demonstrates that there is no such thing as the status quo or staying at the same level. If you develop a muscle, it grows stronger. If you don't use it, it doesn't stay the same—it atrophies. If you use your brain for new experiences, you will grow new pathways called dendrites. If you don't, your brainpower does not stay the same—it will diminish. "Use it or lose it" is more than an idle expression.

Relationships that we pay attention to expand;

those that we neglect do not stay the same—they fade. Perhaps you have had a friendship that was once strong but now is gone. No blow-up; no decision to part, just a bad case of status quo.

At various stages of life, we come to a fork in the road and have to choose which path we'll take. One is familiar, safe, and nicely paved. The other is a bit trickier. It glows with adventure, excitement, and potential treasures—but it is also unfamiliar, rocky, and a bit threatening. The road to the first path leads to contraction; the second path leads to expansion. Either you stay in your comfort zone and let life pass you by, or you take the risks necessary to move your life forward. The choice is yours alone. So, although too much change can be stressful, too little change will literally bore you to death! To feel young and alive and in sync with your potential, try shaking things up a bit.

Passion for life does not wear out
—it fades from lack of use.

—Suzanne Zoglio

TEN WAYS TO REV THINGS UP TODAY!

These quick-lifts will help to get your motor running and your wheels turning. If your life feels a little stale or you're stuck in a holding pattern, these ideas might be just what you need to jumpstart a new phase of your career, your relationships, or your life. Read over all ten and then pick one that appeals to you. In just a few minutes you'll feel the energy seeping back and a revived aliveness, curiosity, and forward energy.

21 **What's Growing…And What's Stuck**

22 **Explore New Territory**

23 **Take Down That "Over the Hill" Sign**

24 **Dream Your Life Forward**

25 **Don't Wait for a Wake-Up Call**

26 **The Enemy Is Us**

27 **Train to Be a Champion of Change**

28 **Cut One Rope**

29 **Make Room for What You Want**

30 **Keep a List of Firm Intentions**

Quick-Lift 21
WHAT'S GROWING...AND WHAT'S STUCK?

To get off square one and get things flowing again, start by assessing which parts of your life are evolving and which ones have gotten a bit stuck.

- On a card, list your key areas of life satisfaction. Consider physical fitness, emotional well-being, career, relationships, finances, service to others, leisure activities, continued learning, spirituality, legacy. Add any other aspects that are important to you personally.

- To the right of each word write "satisfying" (you're generally happy about this aspect of your life) or "not satisfying" (you want more in this aspect), and "challenging" (still stimulates you to learn and grow) or "not challenging" (you can coast now).

- Star any area that you rated "not satisfying." You have "Y," but you want "X." A strong desire for "X" will motivate you to action.

- Star any area that you rated "not challenging." If an area no longer stretches you, it's actually in decline. Consider what you could do to breathe new life into a job, relationship, or hobby.

None of us is the same today as we were yesterday. To live is to change; to live fully is to transform oneself.

Quick-Lift 22
EXPLORE NEW TERRITORY

For many of us, part of the fun of a vacation is exploring someplace new. Getting away from the ordinary is energizing. When we are tired, we also may be tired of our environment and routine. So, for a mini-charge between vacations, consider doing something a little different.

- If you usually drink coffee, try a special tea or hot chocolate.

- If you normally skip lunch, stop and go out to eat.

- Take a different route to work—the scenic route.

- Listen to five minutes of music that 's not your usual choice.

- Talk to someone you've never actually met, but pass by regularly.

- Pick up a paper you seldom read, and read it from cover to cover.

- Visit a different website or a new chat room.

Exploring something new can be exhilarating. It's the contrast to the norm that usually sparks our interest. You don't have to wait for a vacation on an exotic island to recharge; just add a little "exotic" to your day.

Quick-Lift 23

TAKE DOWN THAT "OVER THE HILL" SIGN

*f you're feeling stuck, it's possible that you have
convinced yourself that it's too late to do something
—change careers, go back to school, make new friends,
develop a talent. Well, think again.*

- Try finishing this sentence: "If it weren't too
  late, I'd probably...."

- Review your list and pick one item that really
  stirs you. Imagine how you'd feel if you actually
  achieved that dream.

- Hang on to that thought—if the gain
  outweighs the pain or effort, you're likely
  to do it.

- Notice which dream-buster excuses pop up
  when you consider doing something new. For
  example: "My significant other won't like it,"
  "I'm too old for that," or "I don't have the
  money." Each time a limiting thought appears,
  quickly substitute an empowering thought
  such as, "I can do anything that I truly desire."

*Success can be the death of passion. If you circle your
wagons to protect what you have, you'll travel in circles
instead of moving forward.*

Quick-Lift 24
DREAM YOUR LIFE FORWARD

When we are children, we dream of experiencing all kinds of things. Then, somewhere between college loans and settling down, we lose enthusiasm for the anything-is-possible world, and start playing "get real" tapes. Yet dreams are the flames that ignite our energy for the journey forward. Lift your life by giving yourself permission to dream.

- Pen and paper in hand, start writing a "dream letter" to a dear friend. Pretend it is two years from now and you are describing your ideal life. Where are you living? What are you doing for a living—that you love so much you can't really call it work? With whom are you sharing your heart? What talent or skills are you developing? What's a perfect day like for you? Write as much as you can in five to ten minutes, then put down your pen. Fold the letter and instead of addressing it to your friend, send it to yourself. When it comes back to you, place it where you will read it often.

Creating a picture of your "dream life" is more than an exercise. The more specific your dreams, the closer they will seem. The closer they seem, the more you will be motivated to pursue them.

Quick-Lift 25
DON'T WAIT FOR A WAKE-UP CALL

We've all used—or at least heard—the expression, "That was a real wake-up call." Associated with a shock of some kind—illness, loss, an accident, or even a tragedy like September 11th, such incidents jar us into a sharper realization of what is most important. Well, you don't have to wait for a wake-up call.

- Imagine you found out that you had six months to live. How would you spend that time? What would you want to accomplish? What would you want to say—and to whom? What would you stop putting off until "someday"?

- If you won the lottery, what good would you do with the unexpected dollars? How would you make a difference? Is there someone you'd help, or a cause that comes to mind? If you could, how would you make the world a better place?

- Now, given your answers to the questions above, what can you do—with the time and resources that you have right now—to honor your priorities? What one step can you take today?

To use each day in meaningful ways is to protect yourself from later regrets.

Quick-Lift 26
THE ENEMY IS US

Sometimes we inadvertently put up roadblocks to a better life. Not consciously, of course, but out of fear of the unknown. We might refuse to ask for help, avoid saving enough money, insist that others won't "let" us, or convince ourselves that we've got it pretty good. If your life has not been moving forward lately, see if your attitude toward change needs adjusting.

- Check your reaction to change in general by listing the first words that come into your head when you read:
  "Change is_____."

- When you're apprehensive about trying something new, are you most likely to:
  a) ignore your fear and plow forward,
  b) acknowledge your fears and prepare,
  c) find a "good excuse" for staying right where you are?

- If you won a scholarship for advanced training in an area you'd love to learn more about, would your first response be:
  a) "No way. You can't teach an old dog new tricks!" b) "Yikes! I haven't been a student for years—it'll be tough."c) "Great. I can't wait."

So, are you change-resistant? If so, remember that awareness is the first step to transformation.

Quick-Lift 27

TRAIN TO BE A CHAMPION OF CHANGE

While change adds zest to life, it is also a bit risky. Most of us fear the unknown and can be lulled into a comfortable, lackluster life. But no change, no gain.

- Change your interaction style—just for today. Push beyond your comfort zone in communications. If you're primarily a talker, listen today. If you're primarily a listener, speak up.

- Risk honest expression—at least once today. Make a phone call right now to tell someone something you've been "meaning" to say. For example, "Thank you," "I'm sorry," "I love you," "I appreciate your friendship," or " I miss you."

- Broaden your learning. Read one chapter of a book on your shelf.

- Try a new activity. Make plans to try your hand at something that now appeals to you.

A fulfilling life often stems from risking something you've got, to acquire something you want.

Quick-Lift 28

CUT ONE ROPE

When you feel stuck, as though you just can't move forward, you may be hanging on to something from your past that is actually holding you back.

- Take inventory of all the names that pop into your head when you ask yourself this question: "Who has disappointed me— recently or in the past?"

- And now—the important part: How did you respond at the time? Express your pain, ask for a new promise, or decide to make things right, or did you silently take the hit?

- It's not too late. Whether the grudge or self-regret is from yesterday or long ago, you can decide to let it go. Write a note expressing how you feel—or felt. You don't have to mail it, just express it, so you can let it go. Then rip up the note.

- If you prefer, close your eyes, and visualize a balloon with your regret inside. When you decide it's time, let go of the string and say, "Goodbye." Notice how free you feel.

Letting go of an old hurt, regret, or limiting belief may be just what you need to free up some energy to move your career or life forward.

Quick-Lift 29
MAKE ROOM FOR WHAT YOU WANT

Most of us have closets, drawers, desks, and file cabinets brimming with stuff that we no longer need: a broken clock that we plan to fix one day, jeans that are a size too small, files from clients we haven't serviced in years, or notes from a course that is no longer even taught. All that clutter can keep us attached to the past. Try clearing out some no-longer-needed stuff, and watch for new things to appear in your life.

- Take a break and clear out one letter of a file drawer. Continue with one letter a day until you reach the Z files.

- Set aside five minutes to organize a drawer. Five minutes and then stop. If it takes longer, come back for another five minutes another day.

- Make a list of things you can give away—to Goodwill, the Salvation Army, or out on the street with a "Free—Take Me " sign.

Perhaps it's the decision to break with the past, or the confidence we get when we no longer feel a need to hoard, but getting rid of the old often attracts something new.

Quick-Lift 30
KEEP A LIST OF FIRM INTENTIONS

When *you're stuck in a rut without much passion, it's often because you don't have anything to look forward to. The antidote is always having something new you want to do right at your fingertips, so you don't default to activities that are no longer meaningful to you. When I first started this practice, I included on my list big goals (attend the opera at La Scala, study cooking in Tuscany, buy an ocean house, fund a house for Habitat for Humanity), moderate goals (visit Santa Fe, adopt a family each Christmas season, learn yoga), and very doable goals (read a book a month, learn Pilates, connect with a friend weekly). What would you like to do?*

- Set a time limit of five minutes. At the top of a sheet of paper write *"I'd really like to...."* That's it. Start writing whatever comes into your head.

- Now look over that list and copy the top twenty that most excite you at the moment onto an index card. Keep that list with you.

- As you complete each desire, cross it off your list, and add another.

Passion for life does not wear out—it fades from lack of use.

PASS THE ANTACID!

CALMING
DOWN

Chapter 4

PASS THE ANTACID!

Your stomach is churning, your head is splitting, and your sense of humor has gone AWOL. Reach for the antacid—you deserve some relief. Then, start converting that negative energy into strategy and action. Anger, worry, and regret won't solve anything, nor will ruminating about a problem for hours. "Easier said than done," you might be thinking. True, it's not easy to break out of the stress response, especially if that's how you've been reacting to challenges for some time, but it can be done. You can train yourself to choose a different response when life throws a few boulders in your path. In deciding your response, consider three things. First, you can alter your physical response to stress (heart rate, blood pressure, etc.) by invoking the relaxation response with meditation, prayer, self-hypnosis, and empowering thoughts. Second, all problems are not "fixable." Some things that we worry about are simply beyond our control. Considering how you can convince an angry customer that you deserve a second chance might be very fruitful, but worrying about whether it's going to rain on your daughter's wedding day is not productive. Some concerns you just have to surrender. Also, sometimes we "overwork" a problem that's already been fixed. If you've apologized, made amends, done whatever you could, let it go. Replaying the whole scene over and over will not help and the regret will just eat away at you. Third, not all problems are your responsibility to fix. Worries about whether your son makes the team, your sister's divorce goes well, or a friend gets a raise he deserves are all out of your sphere of influence. If the problem belongs to someone else, don't steal it. Pray for a positive outcome, provide advice if it is requested, or offer empowering comments, but then let the other person handle it. So when a problem appears, leave your body out of it, fix it (if it's yours to fix), or forget it (if it's already fixed or belongs to someone else).

When life spins out of control, and you find yourself in a crisis, remember the many mountains you have climbed.

—Suzanne Zoglio

TEN WAYS TO CALM DOWN PRONTO!

These quick-lifts will help you reduce any inner turmoil stemming from anger, worry, or regret. Here you'll find options for defusing destructive energy before it takes its toll on your health, relationships, and your sanity! In just a few minutes you'll feel the inner churning settling down and a sense of serenity bubbling up. Read over all ten and then pick one that appeals to you.

31 Let off Steam before You Implode

32 Don't Wait to Exhale

33 Stand up for Yourself

34 Reframe the Problem

35 Get out of the Blame Game

36 Choose Your Response to Offense

37 Keep the Faith

38 Negotiate

39 Focus Outward

40 Climb to the Balcony

Quick-Lift 31

LET OFF STEAM BEFORE YOU IMPLODE

While the fix-it-or-forget-it path to inner peace does not include complaining day after day about the same problem, it can include brief venting as a first step. Authentic expression is a good escape valve for energy that has been bottled up.

- Identify one problem that has your stomach churning right now. Contact a friend (a *close friend*) and gripe and whine for a few minutes. Just being heard will help.

- Or, behind closed doors, indulge in a three-minute pity party all by yourself. Punch a pillow, shed a few tears, or rip up some documents that you no longer need

- Writing can also provide a good escape valve. Put pen to paper, set a timer for three minutes and just write whatever comes into your head. No punctuation. No censoring. Just stream of consciousness. Get it off your chest, so you can act with a clear head! Then, tear up the pages.

Expressing negative energy is like washing a wound before you bandage it. Skip the cleansing and you end up with a festering sore.

Quick-Lift 32
DON'T WAIT TO EXHALE

W_hen your stomach is churning, your pulse is racing, and your mind has locked into a defensive mode, you can bet you've shifted into the stress response. One way to reduce a rapid heartbeat, increased blood pressure, sweaty palms, etc. is to slow your system down with focused steady breathing._

- Sit in a chair with your spine straight and your feet on the floor. Close your eyes, if you wish. Inhale slowly to the count of six, bringing the air all the way down to your diaphragm. Hold your breath for the count of two, and then slowly release the breath to the count of six, letting the muscles in your neck and shoulders relax. Repeat eight to ten times, or until you feel your system settling down.

- As you exhale slowly, vocalize "ahhh," if you wish...or "phew," "yes," or "okay."

Remember when your mother used to tell you to count to ten? Well, she was wisely coaching you on how to stay in the driver's seat and manage your emotions, instead of letting them manage you.

Quick-Lift 33
STAND UP FOR YOURSELF

The stress response is generally a fear response, and what we fear most is loss of control. So when your stomach is churning, take charge of something— anything—to remember your power and ability to cope.

- Make a decision right now about a personal preference. It might be where you'll eat, what movie you'll see, the color of the new carpeting, or what time you'll set your alarm for tomorrow. Just do it.

- Express an opinion that you have been keeping to yourself to keep the peace.

- Say "no" to a request—just to practice your assertiveness.

- Let someone know if they recently stepped on your toes, and establish boundaries for future interactions.

When you're all worked up, chances are that you can't control something. Get back at the helm even for a little while with something that's under your control, and you are likely to feel calmer and more able to ride out a squall.

Quick-Lift 34
REFRAME THE PROBLEM

One reason we get so stressed when something goes wrong is that we focus only on what has gone wrong. We wish it hadn't happened and mumble about our rotten luck. Instead, try reframing a problem situation to see if there is any possible good in it.

- Try looking at a current problem from a glass-half-full point of view. For example, if the problem is a cancelled appointment, you might have more time to prepare or to meet a friend for dinner. If the problem is you lost your temper, did you learn how NOT to negotiate? If you got caught in traffic, might a benefit be that you find time to meditate?

Okay, most of us would prefer that problems wouldn't show up at all, but when they do, see if there isn't a silver lining in there someplace. It cushions the blow if you can identify some unexpected gain from unexpected pain.

Quick-Lift 35
GET OUT OF THE BLAME GAME

"**S**he makes my blood pressure soar." "That jerk ruined my day." "I really messed that up." Thoughts like these signal that you're smack in the middle of a blame game—a game that you are certain to lose. The time you spend blaming yourself or someone else is time you could be spending on what to do next.

- What's one thing you've been blaming yourself or someone else for lately—so much so that you haven't spent much time looking for a solution?

- Right now, decide to shift to solution thinking with thoughts such as: "Okay, this is the situation. No matter who or what caused it, it is. Now, what can I do to move forward?"

You can't undo what has already been done, and certainly you can't control how others behave. But one thing you can influence is what YOU do next. When the milk is spilled, don't look for the culprit. Just mop it up and pour some more.

Quick-Lift 36
CHOOSE YOUR RESPONSE TO OFFENSE

*I*f *you live long enough you will encounter tactless people, ungrateful bosses, or insensitive family members. Your choice is to **react defensively** from a place of fear, hurt, and anger, or **respond deliberately** from your center of power.*

- *Express yourself.* Tell the offender how her behavior or statement affected you, using a constructive "I message" that includes impact, offending behavior, and your request. For example, "I was so embarrassed when you told the group how I messed up. In the future I'd prefer you let me share my own mistakes."

- *Forgive the offense silently.* Chalk the offense up to human error, remembering two things: you are not so different from the offender since you probably have caused someone similar distress at some point in your life, and the person may not have had malicious intent, just a lack of skill or insight. Try forgiving both the offender and yourself.

- *Decide not to take offense in the first place.* Realize the comment or action has little to do with you and much more to do with the other person's needs. Try a little empathy.

Offense can be found everywhere or nowhere, depending on who's doing the looking. Make it a practice to always assume positive intent.

Quick-Lift 37
KEEP THE FAITH

Fear and doubt can undermine your faith—in God, yourself, or in your ability to cope. When you meet with one of life's inevitable challenges, stop for a few minutes to reaffirm your faith. The whirling dervish will settle down.

- Repeat an affirming message, such as: *"It'll all work out—it always does"* or your favorite.

- Recite a favorite prayer or this well-known Serenity Prayer: "God give me the strength to accept the things I cannot change, the courage to change the things I can, and the wisdom to know the difference."

- Read an inspiring quotation, such as this one from Dag Hammarskjöld, former secretary general of the United Nations: *"Never measure the height of a mountain until you reach the top. For it is only then that you will see how small it really is."*

A small crack in confidence can grow into full-blown anxiety if left unchecked. Shore yourself up with affirmation, prayer, and inspiration.

Quick-Lift 38
NEGOTIATE

When you're all worked up emotionally, there's a good chance that you're upset because your needs are not being met or someone is not behaving according to your expectations. Instead of losing any more energy on what "should" have gone differently, put your energy into getting what you want.

- Think of a situation that has you upset. What has someone done (or not done) that you wish they hadn't?

- Now, translate that into what you *do* want— a request.

- Consider what the other person really wants.

- Decide what you're willing to give to get what you want—if necessary.

- Now, schedule a meeting to discuss your concerns with the other person—to "negotiate."

Quite often all we have to do to get our needs met is to know what we want, know what others want, and be willing to work for a solution that benefits all parties.

Quick-Lift 39
FOCUS OUTWARD

W_hen we worry about going broke, getting sick, or losing face, our focus is on ourselves. One way to reduce worrying is to shift gears, and focus on how you can help someone else._

- Who among those closest to you is dealing with a health issue, unemployment, family concerns, or some other loss? Do something that you think will help—something that you can do right now. A note of encouragement? An invitation to lunch? A little gift?

- If you could rid the world of one problem, what would it be? AIDS? Child abuse? Battered women? Homelessness? Illiteracy? What truly touches you? Do something on behalf of that cause right now. Call for a brochure. Send a check. Check an Internet site. Sign up to volunteer next weekend. Give in a small way to chip away at a big problem.

When you find a way to improve someone's day, two things will happen: 1) You'll forget your own worries for a while, perhaps even putting them in better perspective, and 2) You'll feel a rush of confidence as you make a difference in someone's life.

Quick-Lift 40
CLIMB TO THE BALCONY

When we are anxious and worried, we often lose perspective. We get so caught up in our present challenge that we forget how many times similar events have worked out just fine in the past. We fail to remember how many storms we have weathered successfully.

- Pretend you are high on a balcony where you can look back over the last few months or even years. Can you see all of the rough spots, challenges, pain, and difficult times that you have survived?

- How did you cope with each of them? What helped you to get through those times successfully?

- Now, in the scope of things—where does your current situation fit? Is it the worst thing you've faced to date—something that you've been "training" to handle for years? Or is it similar to a few you've weathered before? Or —now that you think about it—is it not quite as bad as other situations you've handled?

When life spins out of control, and you find yourself in a crisis, remember the many mountains you have climbed.

Chapter 5

I HAVEN'T GOT A CLUE!

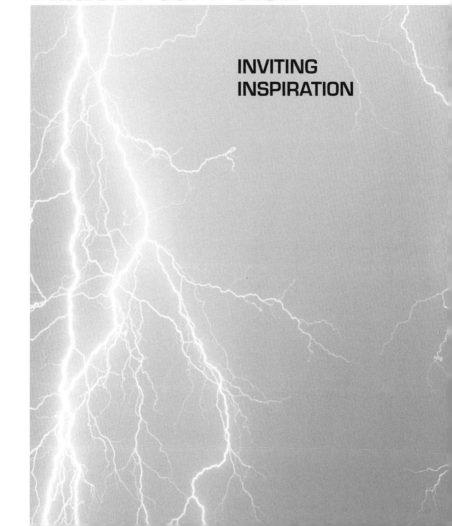

**INVITING
INSPIRATION**

Chapter 5
I HAVEN'T GOT A CLUE!

Have you ever had to create a response, generate a solution, or come up with an innovation ASAP? If so, you know the pressure. It seems just when we need it most, our creative mind goes on vacation. So we try—and we try again. But the harder we try to invent something brilliant, the more drained we become and the more elusive the answer seems. When you concentrate too hard on the right answer, you block your inner genius and lock out your muse.

In Greek mythology muses were any of the nine sister goddesses presiding over song, poetry, and the arts and sciences. Daniel Webster defines a muse as "an inspiration...a guiding genius." Every writer, dancer, artist, musician, builder, parent, businessperson, or teacher knows that there are days when your muse is very much present—and there are days when she goes into hiding. The key to great ideas is the proper care and feeding of your muse.

Like any good friend, your muse will leave you alone when you're hassled or hurried. If your day is chock full of tasks, distractions, worry, and such—she simply won't appear. To coax your muse out, prepare a welcoming place for her—a place where she can visit with you alone and be assured that you will hear her whispered wisdom. No television, radio, phones, or computers. Sit quietly, go for a run, take a shower, or dig in your garden. Or find time to lighten up, laugh, and play with your muse for a while. She loves it when you are spontaneous and joyful, and will generate plenty of inspiration when you are in such an unguarded state. Be curious. Have fun. Be silly. Go out on a limb. Make sure that the activity you choose muffles your mind chatter and allows you to hear the whispers of wisdom from within.

When you are looking for inspiration,
leave your ego behind,
and let your child lead.

—Suzanne Zoglio

TEN WAYS TO INVITE INSPIRATION INSTANTLY!

These quick-lifts will help you find your muse when she seems to be missing. When you are stumped for an idea, fresh out of creative options, or searching for a way out of a dilemma, try one of these block-busting breaks. Read over all ten and then pick one that appeals to you. In just a few minutes your muse will come out of hiding and spark your imagination. Soon the ideas will be flying!

41 Find Your Muse in Nature

42 Turn Complaints into Questions

43 Stimulate Your Inner Artist

44 Take a Play Break

45 Get out of Your Head

46 Change Your Point of View

47 Make Metaphors Work for You

48 Begin with Desired Outcomes in Mind

49 Play Beat the Clock

50 Use Your Brain Trust

Quick-Lift 41
FIND YOUR MUSE IN NATURE

When your muse seems to have disappeared, look for her in nature. She loves the out-of-doors and frequently waits for you there.

- Find a patch of grass, sprawl out on your back, and look for pictures in the clouds. Look for whole scenes to emerge and recede with the shifting wind. Allow your mind to see solutions where you never looked before.

- Step outside or open a window and listen to the sounds surrounding you. Are birds singing, squirrels chattering, or perhaps a dog barking? Is rain splattering, wind howling, or ice dripping off a gutter? Can you hear a pigeon cooing? Just for a moment, turn off the noise inside your head and focus on outer sounds. Now that your muse has your attention, she may slip in an idea.

- Go for a walk, and look for natural expressions of creation. Beauty and order are everywhere.

As you pay attention to the miracles of creation, you will be reminded of how effortless beauty can be. A blade of grass does not try to grow; a bird does not wrack its brain for a tune; a spider does not labor over its intricate web. Like you, all they have to do is not block what comes naturally.

Quick-Lift 42

TURN COMPLAINTS INTO QUESTIONS

Complaints are statements of defeat. They drain energy, stifle creativity, and block suggestions. Questions, on the other hand, stimulate the creative brain by moving our attention from passive acceptance to the realm of possibilities. Questions make us solution-focused; complaints just make us depressed. The next time you hear a complaint (yours or anyone else's), gently turn it into a question.

- Just for today, if you catch yourself grumbling: "Everyone's in a rotten mood today," lead your brain on a hunt for a solution by asking: "I wonder how I could lighten things up around here?" or "What would lift this dark cloud?"

- If you hear someone whining: "They never listen to suggestions from the field," don't commiserate. Instead, empower your colleague by sending the complaint back in the form of a question. When you do so, you are showing confidence in them to do something about the situation. You might ask, "What do you think would get their attention—the money we'd save or outperforming the competition?"

Complaints drain the brain and sour the spirit; questions make problem solving more of a game.

Quick-Lift 43
STIMULATE YOUR INNER ARTIST

You can usually coax your muse out of hiding by engaging in an artistic endeavor. Since she gets bored with an ordinary, paint-by-numbers kind of day, consider taking an artist's break.

- Recite a poem. Even if you haven't read a poem since grade school, find one on your bookshelf, the Internet, or from a friend. When your spirit gets trodden with the weight of the day, let the rhythm of the words or the imagery lift you up before you attempt to solve a problem.

- Take a "tour" of great paintings. Whether they are hanging on your walls, in a beautiful book, or available for viewing on the Internet, fine art will stimulate your passion. You'll move from your left-brain/analytical side, through your heart, to your right-brain/creative side. This is where your muse will join you.

- Listen to five minutes of opera, jazz, classical, or whatever music enlivens your soul.

- Move to music. Hum a waltz and dance around your office (perhaps you'd better close the door!), or clap out a march and strut your stuff. Yes, you might feel foolish at first, but not when that great idea appears!

Open your heart to any art form and you open the door to your own creativity.

Quick-Lift 44
TAKE A PLAY BREAK

*Y*oungsters use their imagination without coaxing.
*They entertain themselves for hours with fantasies,
games, and playmates of their own making. They don't
worry about looking foolish or being realistic. Try it.*

- Make a paper airplane, redesigning it three
  times for greater distance. Invite a few
  companions to join you and do some flight-
  testing together

- Fold a sheet of white paper and cut out
  various corners, making a gorgeous snowflake.

- Using one colored marker draw a rainbow of
  many shades and textures by varying the
  position and pressure of the marker. See how
  many "colors" you can create from one.

- Make a paperclip sculpture that stands on its
  own, or a mobile that you add to often.

- Write a variation on a nursery rhyme, using
  people you know for the characters.

- Compose a "song" about your last great mood,
  putting words to a familiar tune.

*When you are childlike, you open the floodgates on new
ideas. Your inner critic won't like it, but your inner genius
will be thrilled.*

Quick-Lift 45

GET OUT OF YOUR HEAD

Have you ever noticed how great ideas have a way of showing up when you least expect them? You can wrack your brain for hours and find no answer, then go take a shower and be hit with the perfect solution. If what you need is an inspired idea, stop thinking for a few minutes.

- Shake it off. Just like a dog coming in from the rain, shake your whole body from head to tail.

- Reverse the flow. Slowly bend down to touch your toes (bend your knees slightly, if it's more comfortable). Now just hang there, like a Raggedy Ann or Andy doll. Starting at the bottom of your spine, slowly roll back up to standing—one vertebra at a time.

- Get both sides of your brain going. Standing tall, raise your left knee up and touch it with your right bent elbow. Down. Other side. Raise your right knee up and touch it with your left bent elbow.

When you stimulate different parts of your brain, you open up passageways for information to travel. Soon you'll be cross-pollinating from knowledge, experience, and imagination.

Quick-Lift 46

CHANGE YOUR POINT OF VIEW

I once heard a speaker say, "The stand you take often depends upon where you sit." The opinions we espouse and the solutions we suggest are filtered through a very personal lens. To find fresh solutions, see things anew by changing your point of view—literally and figuratively.

- Change your "thinking" space. Move to a different room. Sit in a different chair. Face a different compass direction. Brighten or soften the light.

- Consider a dilemma you currently face. Imagine how Attila the Hun, Mother Theresa, or the Great Houdini would handle it.

- Think of someone whom you admire. How would he or she approach the issue you're considering?

- How would those who will be affected by the decision like to see it resolved?

Einstein wrote, "Problems cannot be solved at the same level of awareness that created them." If you can suspend your own view long enough to see things in a different light, solutions formerly obscured suddenly appear.

Quick-Lift 47

MAKE METAPHORS WORK FOR YOU

One way to generate ideas is to look for comparisons to other situations. That does not mean that the ideal solution will be the same, but the source of the solution might be the same or the type of solution might be similar.

- Does your current challenge remind you of any other challenge that you have faced in the last year? In what ways is it similar?

- If this dilemma were an animal, what animal would it be, and how would you tame it?

- Suppose your problem were a weather event. Would it be like a spring rain, tropical downpour, hurricane, tornado, blizzard, or blistering heat wave? How would you cope?

Making comparisons between unlike things is one way to stimulate your creativity and think in the realm of infinite possibilities.

Quick-Lift 48
BEGIN WITH DESIRED OUTCOMES IN MIND

O*ften when we're stuck for inspiration on what to do next, it's because we're focusing on what to DO next. For a clear stream of inspired ideas, try focusing on your goal instead of on how you will achieve it.*

- For whatever problem you need to solve just now, describe the best possible outcome. Pretend you have three wishes, and you need to be very specific. What tangible results do you hope to see? How do you want each of the affected parties to feel? How do you want to feel?

- When you don't know the specifics of what you really want, try focusing on "the best result for all concerned at the best possible time."

When you know where you want to go, your intuition will provide the best route.

Quick-Lift 49
PLAY BEAT THE CLOCK

I f you have ever had a great idea rejected as "not practical," "unaffordable," or "already tried," you know what it's like to be censored. Someone asks for ideas, you offer your best, and before your great idea is fully explored, some naysayer shoots it down. Even worse, you might censor yourself. An idea pops into your mind, and before you even share it, you hear a little voice shouting, "too dumb," "too risky," "too boring," or the like. You can beat both internal and external censors—and generate a whole stream of ideas—by playing beat the clock.

- Set a timer for three to five minutes. Write down—as rapidly as you can—every idea that pops into your head.

- Don't evaluate or reject anything. Build on ideas—variations on a theme, so to speak.

- Keep writing until your timer goes off.

- Now eliminate anything illegal, immoral, or a threat to your health, and decide which of the remaining ideas sounds best to you.

This brainstorming technique encourages lots of creative ideas in a brief period of time **before** *you evaluate which ideas will work best. In groups this is particularly powerful, because evaluating ideas as you go limits participation and encourages premature decision-making.*

Quick-Lift 50
USE YOUR BRAIN TRUST

hen your search for a solution begins to drain your energy, it's time to tap your brain trust. We all have around us a team of geniuses—just waiting to be asked for their ideas. Coworkers, bosses, spouses, children, siblings, friends, and family all have the potential of sharing exactly the idea that you need at any given moment. You just have to ask.

- Who helps you solve your own problems just by listening intently?

- Given the issue you're wrestling with, who has related practical experience?

- Who has NO experience related to the issue, but has great ideas, in general?

- Who would be so flattered that he'd give you full attention?

- If you put your ego aside, whose opinion would you really like to have?

- Do it—now!

No one succeeds all alone; let the ideas of others lift you to your highest potential.

Chapter 6

IS THIS ALL THERE IS?

CREATING
MEANING

Chapter 6
IS THIS ALL THERE IS?

Have you ever been exhausted at the end of the day, but at a loss to explain just why? You know you were busy, but wonder if it was worth the effort. Thoreau once wrote, "It is not enough to be busy...the important question is: 'What are we busy about?'" In our busy-is-better society, we might all benefit from asking that question. Most of us move so quickly through our to-do lists that we don't even stop for a breath when one task is done, before tackling the next one. We often spend so much time doing what we "should," that we are too tired to enjoy ourselves even when we can. We frantically race through our days reacting to requests and putting out fires and then zone out at night. Contrast that to times when you couldn't wait to get up in the morning, had energy for relationships at night, and looked forward to volunteering for a cause you believe in. What happened?

If things seem a bit disappointing and you're wondering if life is passing you by, you may be trapped in a "have-to" mindset. Your thoughts may sound like these: "I have to do this, but I don't enjoy it anymore." " I have to do this, but I'm not using my real talents." "I have to do this, but I'm not making any real difference." "I have to do this, but it's too hard." "I have to do this, but it's not challenging anymore."

Knowing what you want, doing what you love, making a difference, taking care of yourself, and continuing to grow all add meaning to life. If you find yourself wondering, "Is this all there is?" it's probably time to revisit your preferences, fine-tune your priorities, and make more choices that feel right from the inside out.

When you are being the person you aspire to be, you are fulfilling your personal destiny.

—Suzanne Zoglio

TEN WAYS TO CREATE MORE MEANING!

These quick-lifts will help you to add joy and purpose to your life. Through loving and learning, we find more meaning. So the focus here is on using each day in ways that fill you up and allow you to leave a legacy. Read over all ten and then pick one that appeals to you. In just a few minutes you'll feel more in sync with your higher self.

51 **Check Your Inner Compass**

52 **Learn from Your Heroes**

53 **Make Room for Your Big Rocks**

54 **Consider Your Legacy**

55 **Make a Difference in an Instant**

56 **Put Your Money Where Your Heart Is**

57 **Feed a Passion**

58 **Celebrate Achievements**

59 **Keep a P.O.B. File**

60 **Practice Evening Acknowledgment**

Quick-Lift 51
CHECK YOUR INNER COMPASS

Ever notice how challenging days just seem to spiral out of control? One misstep leads to another and soon your day is in the pits. Perhaps you misplace your keys, skip breakfast, and hit a detour that makes you late. Or in your rush, you leave behind the report you need, forget to pick someone up, or lock your kids out of the house (and then have to make arrangements for a rescue). What can you do? Start—or restart—each day with clarity.

- Awaken ten minutes earlier than usual, or try this centering break at noon.

- Close your eyes, take a few deep breaths, and pose this question: *What do I really want?*

- Now, turn your attention to your breathing. As you exhale, repeat a mantra, if you wish.

- When ten minutes are up, jot down any thoughts that pop into your head. Don't worry if an "answer" does not immediately appear. Just asking is often enough to set your internal compass for the day.

Instead of immersing yourself in morning news, traffic jams, and cell phones that don't sleep, start each day with authentic focus. Connecting with your core provides an anchor all day.

Quick-Lift 52
LEARN FROM YOUR HEROES

The people you most admire can shed light on your core values and the kind of person you aspire to be. If you feel a bit "underwhelmed" with your life, it might be because you have lost sight of the person you have always intended to be. See what your heroes have to say about you.

- When you were young you probably dreamed of being someone you thought was great: a doctor, your mom, Superman, a teacher? Today, who is on your short list of "most admired"—dead or alive?

- Pick one of your heroes and jot down three adjectives that describe that person.

- However you answered, you probably uncovered three traits that you would really like to develop (or honor) more in yourself. What action can you take today that would reflect one or more of those traits? Start being more of the person you aspire to be!

When you are being the person you aspire to be, you are fulfilling your personal destiny.

Quick-Lift 53
MAKE ROOM FOR YOUR BIG ROCKS

popular story describes a time-management professor who demonstrates the importance of prioritizing by filling a five-gallon mason jar with fist-size rocks and asking the class if the jar is full. Since another big rock wouldn't fit, the class answers, "yes." However, the professor proceeds to pour a pitcher of gravel, then sand, and finally water into the jar before it is finally full. The point of the story is not that you can cram much more than you ever dreamed into any given day. The point is this: "If you don't put your big rocks in first, the fillers of life will take up your day and you won't fit your big rocks in at all."

- Take a minute to jot down five areas of your life that are most important to you at this time. You might consider financial security, career, health, spouse, family, friends, emotional well-being, continued learning, spirituality, community service, fun, travel, or anything that you think of as a priority.

- Of your five most important life areas, which one needs more attention at this time? Do one thing related to your "big rock" right now.

*Do something you **choose** to do early each day—for yourself or someone else. When you do what is meaningful to you, you heighten your personal integrity.*

Quick-Lift 54
CONSIDER YOUR LEGACY

Most of us want to make a difference in the lives of others, especially for those people and causes we care about deeply. We want to know that when we're gone, others will remember us kindly, build on what we've contributed, and be better off because of us. A little voice may be asking, "What difference am I making? How will I be remembered when I'm gone? Where have I used the gifts I've been given?" Instead of letting that little voice drone on in the back of your head, turn up the volume, and take a few minutes to consider your legacy.

- How would you like people to describe you after you're gone? Take one small action right now that reflects that trait.

- When you are drawing your last breath, what do you hope you will have done? Take one step—right now—on behalf of that dream.

- If you could be remembered for making the world a better place, what cause would you like to support? Do one thing today on behalf of that mission.

When we're wondering about whether or not our daily efforts are worth it, our legacy might be at the core of that concern. If you knew today was going to be your last, how would you spend it?

Quick-Lift 55
MAKE A DIFFERENCE IN AN INSTANT

When you're wondering if anyone would care if you suddenly disappeared, it's a sure sign that you want to count—to be appreciated. Heighten your sense of purpose by making a difference in someone else's life—instantly.

- Give time to a child today—with a smile, a hug, a story, or a compliment.

- Call an emergency housing shelter, find out what they need, and post it on a bulletin board at work, or email the requests to family and friends.

- Speak up for someone who is not present. Squelch a rumor; suggest that person's strength.

- Dash off a letter to a newspaper editor on behalf of a cause you care about.

- Send someone a thank-you note.

In an instant, you can give a gift that makes the difference between fear and confidence, feeling loved and feeling alone, or knowing hope and knowing despair.

Quick-Lift 56
PUT YOUR MONEY WHERE YOUR HEART IS

Give generously to whatever touches your heart, investing in what feels right to you. Regardless of how great or small your wealth, one way to make each day meaningful is to give something away.

- Go online and donate to the Hunger Site.

- Drop a few coins in a change box at a restaurant.

- Arrange for a charitable deduction to be taken directly from your paycheck.

- Go without one "extra" today and donate that money to your place of worship.

- Send an anonymous gift to a friend or family member.

- Call your lawyer and include a good cause in your will.

It is often written that what goes around comes around. Give generously with no strings attached and you will usually take away much more than you give.

Quick-Lift 57
FEED A PASSION

When you engage in an activity that you really enjoy, time seems to fly. The moment is meaningful; you feel fully alive. Taking time to share what you're good at, develop what interests you, or engage in what brings you joy adds meaning to life.

- Keep a book related to one of your passions handy. Then even when you can't actually go fishing, paint, ride your bike, or write, you can still feed your passion with quick images or bits of information.

- Music and audio books make for great quick-lift breaks. If you have no time for the opera, listen- to one aria on your Walkman. If learning about World War I is your passion, listen to one chapter of a related book on tape.

- Just discussing your passion with another aficionado can revive your spirit. Call another pilot, discuss flowers with another gardener, or visit a parenting chat room online for a few minutes.

Feed your soul's desire—even if only briefly—and see if you don't change your tune. Instead of Peggy Lee's "Is That All There Is?" you may find yourself singing Patti LaBelle's "I've Got a New Attitude."

Quick-Lift 58
CELEBRATE ACHIEVEMENTS

If you go from "to-do" to "to-do," without any pause for applause, you could end up feeling overworked, underappreciated, and even incompetent. We all need to know our efforts are actually paying off; otherwise, what's the point?

- What have you accomplished lately that you failed to acknowledge? Did you resolve a conflict, finish a project, close a deal, or other wise achieve something you set out to do?

- Stop now and celebrate. Treat yourself to a special beverage, take your break in a different place, or call a good friend to share the news

- Find a mirror, look at your reflection, and say, "Hey, great job. I'm proud of you!"

- When others congratulate you today on a job well done, take a moment to let their words sink in. It's easy to brush off compliments and minimize our own efforts. Instead, be open to sincere expressions of respect and appreciation. Let the words affirm the impact that you have made.

A little self-pat on the back will go a long way toward reinforcing the fact that your efforts have been worthwhile. Bask in the glory of success—for at least a few minutes every day.

Quick-Lift 59
KEEP A P.O.B. FILE

he expectancy theory of motivation explains that we will be motivated to work at something if we expect two things: 1) that we will succeed and 2) that our success will result in a reward that is personally meaningful. Belief that you will succeed is based primarily on past experience.

- Take a file folder, shoebox, or large envelope and label it P.O.B. (for pat on back). Write "Success!" on the top of a few blank index cards, and place them in your file.

- Now, what have you accomplished recently? Note each achievement on one of your "Success!" cards, date it, and file it in your P.O.B. file.

- Look for any recent notes of appreciation from someone you helped, and add them to your P.O.B. file also. When you take a risk, learn something new, or break an old habit, file a success card as well.

- Now put your P.O.B. file in a handy place. The next time you find yourself wondering if you're using your days in meaningful ways, pull it out—and look back on your successes.

Reviewing past successes helps keep a positive perspective regarding the future. You'll probably feel more resilient when you realize how far you have come and all the good that you have done.

Quick-Lift 60
PRACTICE EVENING ACKNOWLEDGMENT

There's nothing better to pump up your sense of purpose than to recognize your daily progress. However, if you're like most people, you go to sleep focusing on all the things you didn't get done today—and all the mistakes you made. If the last thoughts you have before you drift off to sleep are about "lack"—what you didn't accomplish, what you didn't receive, or what went wrong—you won't awaken very inspired in the morning. Instead, try to get in the habit of going to sleep with positive thoughts dancing in your head.

- Just before you go to sleep tonight, answer these four questions:

  1. In what moments today was I the person I aspire to be?

  2. What did I accomplish that was important to me?

  3. Where did I make a difference in someone's life?

  4. What pleasant surprises came my way?

Begin your practice of "Evening Acknowledgment" tonight, or try it right now about your day so far. Do it at noon and you will approach the rest of your day with the energy that comes from knowing that you are using your day in meaningful ways.

Chapter 7

IT'S LONELY IN HERE!

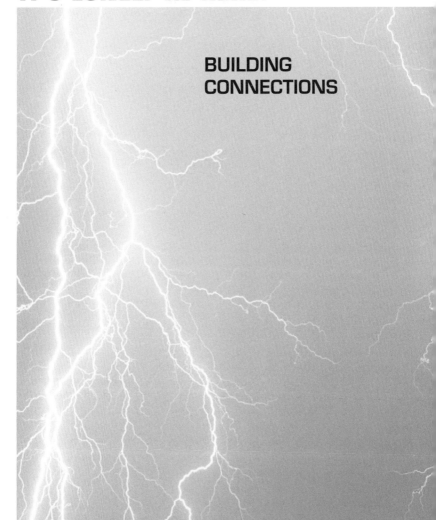

**BUILDING
CONNECTIONS**

Chapter 7
IT'S LONELY IN HERE!

There are times when we all feel a bit disconnected from the rest of the world. It might seem as though no one is in your corner ready to back you up or that few people really want to hear about your joys and sorrows. Perhaps you have fewer and fewer friends whose company you seek and who in return seek you out.

Maybe you've had your nose to the grindstone for far too long and have gotten into a rut of all work and no play. Maybe you've been dealing with feelings that cannot be shared easily, or have been so stressed out that you can focus only on licking your wounds.

Whatever the reason, when you feel adrift—separated from colleagues, family, God, or even your true self—it's time to assess what's happening, reach out to others, and respond when others reach out to you.

That may be easier said than done, because disconnects are often part of a vicious cycle. When we don't feel good about ourselves it's normal to withdraw from others. That increased separation makes us feel even less confident, so we withdraw further. To break the cycle, you've got to step up to the plate, take responsibility for the situation you've helped to create, and do something different.

One way to strengthen a relationship is to "show up." To make time for the care and feeding of the connection is to nurture it not just when it's convenient, but when it needs it. Another way is to create reciprocity by sharing and listening, giving and receiving, and initiating and responding. Intimacy always travels a two-way street. A third way is to be open without judging. To be your true self, yet accepting of others, can be tricky business. It means you share your insight without needing to be right, and you behave as you choose without insisting that others follow your rules. In ways large and small, you can strengthen relationships by giving of your time and your heart.

The first rule for enhancing relationships is to show up—physically present, mentally tuned in, and emotionally engaged.

—Suzanne Zoglio

TEN WAYS TO CONNECT IN SECONDS!

These quick-lifts will help you to feel like part of something larger than yourself. When it seems you are all alone with your troubles and joy, and you'd like to feel more connected, these relationship lifts will help you to do so. Read over all ten and then pick one that appeals to you.

61 Be Accessible

62 Speak Your Truth

63 Reconnect with Your Faith

64 Give of Your Gifts

65 Listen with Your Heart

66 Practice Your Godparent Act

67 Put Away the Gavel

68 Be Amenable

69 Receive Graciously

70 Stay Plugged In

Quick-Lift 61
BE ACCESSIBLE

If your door is always closed, your answering machine always on, and your "visiting hours" limited, you send a message of disinterest. Walling yourself off for months at a time makes it unlikely that many folks will be waiting in line when you suddenly feel the urge to connect. Repeated interactions—regardless of how brief—are the basis of lasting connections.

- First, take stock of how you might be blocking incoming visits, calls, or networking. For example, are you not taking calls, not returning calls, or sending too-busy-to-visit messages?

- Second, identify what's presently blocking your outgoing visits, calls, or networking. For example, are friends a low priority, do you fear rejection, or are you working 24/7?

- Third, identify one person or group that you'd like to get closer to, and schedule them in right now. The "appointment" you make might be with yourself (i.e., call my brother every Sunday starting this week), or it could be agreed upon with the other party as well (i.e., meet for lunch the first Thursday of every month).

The first rule for enhancing relationships is to show up—physically present, mentally tuned in, and emotionally engaged.

Quick-Lift 62

SPEAK YOUR TRUTH

Sometimes we feel disconnected because our inside and outside don't match. Perhaps you have fallen into the habit of not sharing your true beliefs. You might withhold an opinion to avoid conflict, or suppress gratitude so you won't appear too vulnerable. Failing to speak from the heart, however, makes us feel disconnected from a core part of ourselves.

- List three times recently when you wanted to express a sentiment, but ignored the urge.

- Looking at your list, decide if you still would like to express one of those thoughts or feelings.

- Pick one and do it. Make the call, walk down the hall, send an email, or write a note.

Each time you muffle your inner voice, you chip away at your personal integrity. To feel more in sync, identify any people and situations that seem to coincide with you telling white lies, puffing yourself up, or sitting on your true thoughts. That way, you'll be forearmed next time to speak more honestly.

Quick-Lift 63
RECONNECT WITH YOUR FAITH

Feeling alone can be a sign of weakened or neglected faith. When your belief in the divine is strong, you don't feel empty or abandoned; you feel full and supported.

- Have you ever found comfort in the words of others? Perhaps it was when you faced a difficult time, were afraid, or were very disappointed. The words might have been a short prayer, psalm, inspirational quote, or thoughts from a friend. Write down those words that once gave you strength and hope on an index card or slip of paper.

- Keep that card with you today. Prop it up by your telephone, slip it into a shirt pocket, set it beside your computer, or tape it to your refrigerator.

- Every time you see the card, take one deep cleansing breath, and then read the words silently or aloud, allowing your spirit to be uplifted.

We all need to be reminded from time to time of the presence of a much greater force. It is then that we feel blessed, protected, and connected to universal love.

Quick-Lift 64
GIVE OF YOUR GIFTS

W *hen you're feeling separated, try shifting your focus to the needs of someone else, and on how you might be able to help. As you focus on giving to others, you'll ignite a cycle of prosperity that will flow back to you immediately.*

- What are you good at and love learning more about? Could it be motorcycles, marketing, wellness, gardening, fashion, communication, or something else?

- Who (individual or group) could use what you're good at? A charity, a friend or family member, a neighbor, or a colleague?

- How would you enjoy using your talent to help out? Do you like teaching, fundraising, leading, organizing, networking, or something else?

- Take one step right now to get that ball rolling. For example: you could mark your calendar, make a call, or share your idea with a friend.

When you share yourself with someone else, you are welcomed into the heart of humanity.

Quick-Lift 65
LISTEN WITH YOUR HEART

rying to connect with another by way of the spoken word alone is like trying to climb a mountain with only a rope. Words can be helpful, but they are only one tool. To touch another person meaningfully, we also need intuition and empathy.

- Thinking of someone with whom you'd like to connect more closely, imagine your last conversation. What did the person's voice, pace, or intonation indicate to you? What "signals" did you pick up on that were never spoken?

- How much did you learn about what's going on in the other person's life vs. how much you talked about your own?

- Did you demonstrate that you were really listening, by responding before you changed the subject or asking a follow-up question?

- Did you show empathy for the person by reflecting their feelings or sharing a time when you experienced a similar feeling?

- Did you validate the person's importance to you? For instance, did you sound pleased to hear from them, mention how good it was to connect, listen in an unhurried manner, or offer a compliment, etc.?

Listen with your ears if you want to be right; listen with your heart if you want to connect.

114

Quick-Lift 66
PRACTICE YOUR GODPARENT ACT

Acts of kindness need not be huge or even time-consuming to lift your day. In a flash, you can act like a fairy godmother (or godfather), granting wishes anonymously to someone who could use a lift. Not for recognition, thanks, or the return of a favor, but just to feel good about extending yourself.

- Provide a well-timed treat: a cup of tea for a colleague who needs a break, a special chocolate bar for a friend who's blue, a take-out lunch delivered to a buried-under colleague, or a cup of chicken soup for some one with the sniffles.

- Leave a message of encouragement: an anonymous note, an uplifting quote, an inspiring book, a tape, a framed poem, or mini-poster—anything that will provide a ray of hope.

- Send a token of beauty: a single flower, scented candle, a special bookmark, a shimmering glass paperweight, or a miniature oil painting— anything that reminds one of life's simple riches.

Commit an act of anonymous generosity and feel the sheer joy of selfless giving.

Quick-Lift 67
PUT AWAY THE GAVEL

Feeling alone and disconnected can be a sign that you set yourself apart from other people, judging them because they are not like you. You might avoid some people because you find them boring, others because they talk too much. Perhaps you think some are selfish and others have no backbone. You cannot be judging and accepting at the same time. When you label someone, you put miles between you and the other person. Drop your judgments of others and notice warmer connections with everyone.

- Think of someone you have disparaged recently—mentally or verbally. Now list all the words that come into your mind when you describe that person.

- Using your list, ask of each word: "What is my evidence of that trait?"

- For each word, recall times when the description might occasionally apply to you.

When you accept others without judgment, you become open to what you have in common, building bridges where voids once existed.

Quick-Lift 68
BE AMENABLE

*I*f things generally have to be done your way, you may
find yourself low on connections. Adults tire quickly of
*having to play by someone else's rules. If department meetings
must always be by your schedule, household chores must
be done your way, the movies you see must be your choice,
or where you eat must be your decision, you will soon find
you have a very limited number of "playmates." Consider
being more amenable in the interest of developing more
mature relationships.*

- Think of someone with whom you'd like a stronger relationship.

- Considering your recent interactions, what were the occasions when you deferred to the other person's needs, interests, suggestions, or schedule? How many of your interactions were clearly driven by your convenience or taste?

- What could you do today to demonstrate respect for the other person's needs? For example, you might contact them at a time convenient to them, offer to meet in their area, suggest they pick a restaurant or movie, allow a chore to be done their way, etc.

*Being amenable to the suggestions of others—not always
insisting that you control the show—demonstrates respect
for the other person and your interest in forging an inter-
dependent relationship.*

Quick-Lift 69
RECEIVE GRACIOUSLY

Asking *for help brings with it a sense of vulnerability that many people find difficult to experience. If you usually are the one in charge, you might find it harder than most people to ask someone for help or even accept it when it is offered. Yet to ask for help is to honor someone else; to receive graciously is to give a gift in return.*

- What kind of help could you use today—a brainstorming partner, another pair of hands, a piece of good advice?

- Given your needs and current situation, who could offer what you need?

- How would you feel if any of those people asked you for help?

- Call one. Call two. Call three, if you're on a roll.

To receive graciously that which another person offers is to give the gift of gratitude and find a place in that person's heart.

Quick-Lift 70
STAY PLUGGED IN

While some connections blow up from a major disagreement or betrayal, many just fade from lack of attention. Trust that was once strong wears thin, and being on the same page does not occur as frequently. If you didn't intentionally let the relationship go, you might have just fallen into the trap of status quo. Like any living thing, interpersonal connections need TLC to thrive. They can dry out occasionally and be revived, but if ignored too long they shrivel up and die.

- Which friendships, business connections, or other relationships are important to you?

- When was the last time you made a "deposit" in each relationship?

- What could you do right now to nurture one relationship?

Consider the care and feeding of close relationships as important as brushing your teeth. If you miss a day, it's no big deal, but if you miss a month, you're on your way to decay.

IF I'M SO SMART, WHY DON'T I KNOW IT?

BOOSTING CONFIDENCE

Chapter 8

IF I'M SO SMART, WHY DON'T I KNOW IT?

We all have days when we brim with confidence and feel prepared to take on whatever challenges come our way. Also, we all have days when we second-guess ourselves. You may wonder if you're ready for more responsibility or if you can handle an unexpected change. Perhaps it's a relationship you're not sure you can manage—or a challenging assign-ment. Whenever fear takes up residence, it stirs the waters of past mistakes. Every slip, miss, and minor faux pas that you haven't thought about in years suddenly reappears—somehow seeming even larger than the first time around.

Suddenly your inner critic takes control of the microphone in your head, relentlessly dishing out deflating remarks such as: "That'll never work." "You can't get it done on time." "Who are you kidding

—you don't have what it takes!" Before you know it, you may even catch yourself voicing similar put-downs out loud: "No way can I do this!" "I'm over my head." "They'll never believe me." We sometimes say things to ourselves that we would never say to a dear friend. If a friend were suffering from an attack of low confidence, you would most likely encourage him or her with comments like: "You've got what it takes—hang in there," or "Remember how well you handled that last big project." We all would do well to use this as a confidence-booster litmus test: if you wouldn't say it to someone you care about, don't say it to yourself. Period.

If you'll listen intently, there is always another voice in your head trying to be heard. "You're ready," it says, "you've handled much bigger challenges. Remember how hard you've prepared." Your coach and your critic are about to go at it. Your job is to turn up the volume on the one that serves your best interests.

Do not wait for others to confirm your worth;
you have all the evidence you need
within yourself.

—Suzanne Zoglio

TEN WAYS TO BOOST YOUR CONFIDENCE!

These quick-lifts will help you to feel more sure of yourself. When you doubt your own gifts, feel like you've met your limits, or generally wonder if you've got what it takes, these breaks will feed your esteem. Read over all ten and then pick one that appeals to you.

71 Keep a Commitment to Yourself

72 Acknowledge Your Gifts

73 Admit You're Not Perfect

74 Talk to Yourself...Nicely

75 Craft a New Loop Tape

76 Send "I Can't" Packing

77 Play Hail to Your Hurdles

78 Take a Learning Break

79 Swim in the Deep End

80 Dust off Your Trophies

Quick-Lift 71
KEEP A COMMITMENT TO YOURSELF

We all make and keep many commitments each day—to friends, family, bosses, and coworkers. It feels good to keep the promises that we make. But in keeping commitments to others we sometimes put off the promises we make to ourselves. You know the ones: "I'll walk two miles tomorrow," "I'll sign up for a smoking cessation class," "I'll call my good friend," "I'll schedule a colonoscopy," "I'll cut down on sugar," "I'll take my vacation this year," "I'll read for one hour every night," or "I'll get a massage." You might even postpone commitments that would enable you to move your career forward, such as: "I'll redo my resume," "I'll call someone to network," "I'll take a skill class," or "I'll start saving so I can start my own business." When you keep a commitment to yourself, your confidence gets a boost.

- List six things you've been meaning to do.

- Pick one thing on your list that you could complete or start in the next fifteen minutes.

- Now, do it.

- When you're finished, check it off your list —with pride!

Keeping promises you've made to yourself—from cleaning the garage to applying for a new job—speaks volumes about your personal integrity.

Quick-Lift 72
ACKNOWLEDGE YOUR GIFTS

Each of us is born with unique gifts. Being aware of those gifts adds to our feelings of self-worth. But often we forget to acknowledge, enjoy, develop, and share our talent with others. You might have pushed your gifts into the background for so long that finding them again will feel like running into a long-lost friend.

- What do you consider three of your positive personal traits? For example, are you creative, honest, sincere, funny, emotionally astute, trustworthy, brave, sensitive, tenacious, intuitive, generous, etc.

- What skill sets have come to you easily most of your life? For example, are you good with numbers, tools, design, selling, teaching, art, athletics, language, coaching, leading, etc.?

If you inventory your positive personal traits and your natural talents on a regular basis, you will remember your inner greatness. And how can you feel insecure at the same time you are feeling great?

Quick-Lift 73
ADMIT YOU'RE NOT PERFECT

Why would admitting that you're not perfect boost your confidence? When you admit a mistake, shortcoming, or lack of information, you allow others to see the "real" you. Then when the sky doesn't fall, you realize that you don't have to hide behind a mask of perfection. In fact, you'll likely find that "perfect" is not necessary, and "really good" is good enough. What a relief—and boost to your confidence.

- What recent mistake or slip-up can you now admit and even laugh about? Seize the next opportunity to do so.

- Would you like to know something, but feel too foolish to ask? Pick up the phone right now, swallow your pride, and ask away.

- What shortcoming do you find it hard to admit? Not good with numbers, uncoordinated, can't carry a tune? Be aware of an opportunity today to spill the beans.

As you accept yourself—warts and all—dropping the mask of perfection, you will find that others will accept you too, perhaps even more lovingly. No one really enjoys a know-it-all.

Quick-Lift 74

TALK TO YOURSELF...NICELY

How often do you talk to yourself—and in what manner? When you make a mistake, do you have a pet name for your bumbling self—perhaps klutz, fool, or worse? When you excel at something without much effort, do you have a favorite disclaimer of your brilliance—such as "it was nothing" or "anyone could have done it"? If so, you may be giving your inner critic too much airtime. It's time to talk to yourself as if you are someone you care about.

- Imagine your best friend just shared with you a regret or fear similar to the one that's on your mind today. "Listen" intently as your friend explains what's made him or her feel this way.

- With compassion, state how you imagine your friend must be feeling.

- What words of encouragement do you have for your friend? Perhaps you'd say: "It'll be all right," "You'll handle it, I'm sure," "I remember you dealing with something like this before," or "It'll be rough, but you'll land on your feet."

- Now, spotlight on you! Mustering up the same compassion you'd have for a friend, offer yourself a few words of encouragement. For example you might try: "It's not what I would have chosen, but I've bounced back before."

When you talk to yourself, always imagine you are talking to a dear friend.

Quick-Lift 75
CRAFT A NEW LOOP TAPE

Nonstop chatter fills our heads all day long. Like shooting stars across the skies, thoughts of all kinds streak across our minds. Certain "loop" tapes play regularly from beginning to end and then repeat over and over again. Negative loop tapes wear down your confidence out of sheer frequency. So take charge of what messages play in your head by creating affirming messages and playing them regularly.

- Think of three adjectives you'd like to be able to say about yourself at this time. Now, use the words you picked to complete this statement: "I am ____, ____, and ____."

- Don't worry about whether or not the statement is true at this time. Just write it down as if it were true, and repeat the statement several times a day. The repetition creates a new positive loop tape.

- Rewrite your daily affirmation with different adjectives whenever you wish. Just remember to keep the statement positive (generous vs. not selfish; calm vs. not nervous, fit vs. losing weight) and in the present (I am vs. I will be or I want to be).

If you tell yourself that you are what you want to be often enough, you will soon believe it, and behave accordingly. We believe what we hear repeatedly, and we become what we believe.

Quick-Lift 76
SEND "I CAN'T" PACKING

Every time you start a thought or phrase with "I can't," you knock your confidence down a peg. If your self-esteem is feeling a bit below par, take stock of how often you block any creative solutions by stopping your mind in its tracks with that dead-end thought of "I can't."

- Just for today, carry an index card with you. Every time you think or say a self-limiting phrase beginning with "I can't..." or "I'll never..." jot down the specific phrase. Then under the phrase, write an empowering statement beginning with "I can if I...." For example, if you wrote: "I'll never get promoted around here," your empowering statement might be: "I can get promoted if I do a bang-up job on this new project." If your limiting statement was "I can't start my own business," your empowering statement might be, "I can start my own business if I find a partner to share the expenses with me," or "I can start my own business if I work for someone else for a year to learn the business."

- Shift all "I can't" statements to "I can if I..." statements and watch your confidence climb.

Think of "I can't" as a pathetic chap who never could do anything. Send him packing, and invite in a world of possibilities with a new friend, "I can if I...."

Quick-Lift 77

PLAY HAIL TO YOUR HURDLES

Even *when we know at our core that we're capable and lovable and worthy of good things coming our way, we can hit a period when one hurdle after another seems to block our path. We may wonder how much more we can take without caving in. That's when it's time to focus on all the hurdles you've cleared in the past.*

- Set a timer for three minutes; poise your pen on paper, and begin. Without lifting your pen from the paper, list the many challenges that you have survived going all the way back to your first week of school when you rode the bus all by yourself. Writing quickly, record —in any order—whatever "successes" pop into your head. They might include projects completed, fears overcome, new things tried, or competitions won.

- When three minutes are up, put your pen down, and review your list.

- As you review your list of challenges met, remember the feeling you had when you completed each—and in what way you grew stronger.

The school of hard knocks builds resiliency. Your history of hurdles demonstrates that you will deal with whatever comes your way—and land on your feet.

Quick-Lift 78
TAKE A LEARNING BREAK

A *ny nagging self-doubts about being over the hill or underskilled tend to fade in proportion to the amount of new information we acquire. Just learning a new word can give you a lift. When you interview a new client, become informed about a world event, or improve your golf swing, the lift can be even better.*

- What would you like to learn more about?

- What learning resources are at your fingertips right now? A mentor, coworker, the Internet, television, radio, magazines, newspapers, books, tapes, or lunchtime seminars?

- Match your interest with the resources and go! Set a time limit—and jump in. Learn one new thing in the next five to ten minutes. Don't worry. If you get hooked, you can always take another learning break tomorrow.

A work in progress is full of potential. Keep learning and you'll always be self-assured.

Quick-Lift 79
SWIM IN THE DEEP END

Remember *the first time you rode a two-wheeler, climbed the high diving board, went up in a plane, interviewed for a job, spoke before a large group, or bought a car by yourself? Risky business, eh? But how did you feel when you moved forward—knees knocking or not—and did that scary thing? If we were charting your level of self-confidence, we would likely see a dip before the action and then a spike right afterward.*

- What would you like to do, but still find a bit too risky? Perhaps you'd like to tell someone how you really feel or admit your career ambitions to your boss. Maybe you'd like to invite a colleague to lunch or take a fitness test. Perhaps you've been toying with the idea of running a marathon, auditioning for a local theater production, or joining your church choir.

- Whatever scary thing you choose, write down how you think you'll feel if you finally do it (i.e., pumped, confident, strong, honest, self-satisfied).

- Keep that feeling in mind, and get going. Do one thing in the next five minutes to set the wheels in motion.

When you do something that stretches you, your confidence grows. You are reminded of your capacity to expand. Every now and then, you've got to swim in the deep end.

Quick-Lift 80
DUST OFF YOUR TROPHIES

When your confidence hits a temporary lull, you can often get a little lift from focusing on mementos of your shining moments. Not that you want to live in the past, but to gain some perspective regarding all that you have done right.

- If you have a memories box, take it out and make yourself a cup of tea to sip as you stroll down memory lane.

- If you're at work, check your surroundings —the team photo from a successful project, the plaque you received for volunteering at the blood drive, the paperweight your assistant gave you for being so kind, the book a coworker left because you had taught her so much, the photo of your family at the cabin you built—or bought—with much effort.

- Take time with each item, and let the reminder of a past success wash over you. Each momento has something to say about who you are, whom you have touched with your life, and who you can become.

As you dust off photographs, certificates, notes, and special little gifts, you'll be reminded of times when it felt great to be in your shoes—and of your potential to feel that way again.

Chapter 9

WHAT IF IT DOESN'T WORK?

**DISCOVERING
COURAGE**

Chapter 9
WHAT IF IT DOESN'T WORK?

Even when you know who you are, what you want, and how to get it, another block may pop up to stop you from living as you wish. It's called risk! Living large is risky business. There is no getting around it. If you want to move forward at work or in life, you will have to shore up your courage and get used to sticking your neck out. As the old saying goes: "No guts, no glory!"

Finding courage and taking risks does not mean that you feel no fear. It just means that you don't let fear paralyze you. As Susan Jeffers' book proclaims in the title, successful people *Feel the Fear and Do It Anyway*. Acknowledge what it is that you fear, examine the probability of it occurring, and consider your possible responses if it does. With analysis and planning you will increase your sense of control, and become more open to taking the risks necessary to move your life forward.

Seeing fear as neither something to ignore nor something to obsess about keeps change-related risk in perspective. Try imagining your fear as a little person, smaller than you, but real all the same. You might "name" your fear so you can understand it better. Then when you want to take a risk, it won't be difficult to visualize yourself taking little fear by the hand and walking forward—in the direction of your goals. There are several actions you can take to restore your energy when anxiety about the future is draining you.

When something you want involves taking a risk, don't ask, "What if it doesn't work?" Instead, ask, "How will I feel if I don't even try?"

—Suzanne Zoglio

TEN WAYS TO DISCOVER COURAGE!

These quick-lifts will help you to go where you want to go even if you're anxious about the outcome. When opportunity knocks, you'll be prepared to mobilize your fear and move forward. Read over all ten and then pick one that appeals to you.

81 **Turn up the Flame of Your Desire**

82 **Picture Your Desired Outcome**

83 **Practice, Practice, Practice**

84 **Coax out Your Papa Bear Fear**

85 **Stop Catastrophizing**

86 **Do the Math**

87 **Build Your Change Muscles**

88 **Create a Courage Timeline**

89 **Lean on Your Team**

90 **Let Others Inspire You**

Quick-Lift 81
TURN UP THE FLAME OF YOUR DESIRE

Remember *when you wanted to play on a team so badly that you endured tryouts, hazing, and grueling practice? Or when you wanted to get married, even though you knew 50 percent of all marriages end in divorce? Maybe you know someone who invested his or her last dollar to start up a small business. What do all of these risks have in common? A burning desire. Try pumping up your courage by focusing on what you really want.*

- What would you try today if you knew you couldn't fail?

- What would it feel like if you succeeded?

- On a scale of one to ten, how badly do you want to succeed?

- What will be the best part of succeeding?

When desire is very strong, we don't spend much time worrying about what can go wrong.

Quick-Lift 82
PICTURE YOUR DESIRED OUTCOME

I f you want to rev up your motivation to achieve a goal,
*frame your desired goal in the positive (i.e., weigh 150,
rather than not be overweight) and create a clear mental
picture of you enjoying your success. For most people,
pictures provide more of an emotional charge than words
alone. Overcome any natural hesitation by posting a
positive image of what your "success" will look like. Every
time you glance at the image representing your reward,
you'll remember how much you want it and you'll be more
energized to satisfy that need.*

- Flip through a magazine until you find a
  photo that represents your reward, if you
  succeed at what you want. Cut it out, post it,
  or keep it in a drawer that you open several
  times a day.

- Take a photo of yourself and paste it on top
  of a picture that symbolizes what you want.

- Sketch a simple picture, using symbols and
  stick figures to form a collage that is symbolic
  of what is waiting for you if you find the
  courage to chase what you want.

*Keep your mind's eye on your desired outcome and you'll
have little time for imagining demons.*

Quick-Lift 83
PRACTICE, PRACTICE, PRACTICE

There is an old joke about Leonard Bernstein: When asked by a tourist how to get to Carnegie Hall, the famous conductor answered, "Practice, practice, practice." The quip may be worn, but the message is just as true today. If you want to move out of your comfort zone into new territory, you've got to put in the rehearsal time. Practice can take many forms.

- Notch up your preparation for whatever risk you want to take. Get advice from mentors, read up on the facts, review strategies that have worked for you before. Your courage will soar.

- Mentally "practice" your success. Close your eyes and visualize getting the new job, completing the project, or handling a difficult discussion. If you play that success movie often enough in your mind, you may soon find your feet following the same path.

- It might even help to visualize what might go wrong, and how you will cope.

Imagining yourself in a risky situation makes it seem as though you have been there before. It doesn't take as much courage to go to a familiar place as one you've never visited.

Quick-Lift 84

COAX OUT YOUR PAPA BEAR FEAR

Sometimes we stall our own progress, rationalizing to cover-up for our fear. When you'd like to make a move, but can't seem to get going, coax your Papa Bear fear out into the open by conducting an escalating-depth interview.

- If you wanted a better job in another city, you might ask: *"What is my biggest concern about moving forward at this time?"* If your answer were, *"Moving the family,"* you'd then ask: *"Why is that a problem?"* If your answer were, *"My spouse loves her job,"* you'd then ask: *"And?"* If your answer were, *"She might decide not to come,"* you'd then ask, *"And?"* again. If your answer were, *"I wouldn't be able to negotiate,"* you'd ask: *"And?"* again. Your answer might be, *"I'd be miserable and all alone."*

In the above example, the fear was of losing a companion. With the core fear out in the light, steps can be taken to reduce the risk (discussion, negotiation, even counseling). Try the same method for something you are reluctant to do using the in-depth interview method.

- *What is one dream you'd like to pursue?*
  What concerns you about the move?
  And? And? And? And?

Once you expose a core concern, you can take steps to deal with it going forward. If you ignore your fears, you'll be left on the platform as the opportunity train pulls out.

Quick-Lift 85
STOP CATASTROPHIZING

*A*ll change involves risk since we cannot predict the impact of the unknown. We can, however, anticipate a reasonable range of possible outcomes. The operative word here is **reasonable**. If you decide to leap over probable outcomes, fast-tracking directly to full-blown catastrophes, you can scare yourself into staying right where you are. If you are prone to exaggerations such as "I'll get killed," "She'll never speak to me again, " or "I'll get fired," you may be a catastrophizer.

- To see if you are catastrophizing about a current situation, use the next two minutes to jot down all the phrases that come to mind when you think about a current concern that might have negative consequences.

- If your responses quickly plummeted from you'd be upset to you'd be ruined to you'd probably die all alone in a box on the street, you're a catastrophizer.

- To shift catastrophic thinking, you must first be aware when such a thought arises. Second, play devil's advocate, asking if the results are really going to be *that* bad. Third, shift your focus from possible risk to probable reward.

It's one thing to consider what might go wrong so you can prepare, and quite another to assume that the worst will happen. One gives you courage; the other makes you weak in the knees.

Quick-Lift 86
DO THE MATH

If you're hesitating to take a risk, it might not be the extreme nature of the consequences that has you stuck, but your certainty that something bad is going to occur. If you are convinced that some undesirable consequence such as looking foolish, getting fired, losing wealth, or being rejected by someone you care about is definitely going to occur, you are not going to take a risk. So take a few minutes right now to consider a risk you'd like to take. Now, imagining all the possible outcomes, what is the likelihood of a negative outcome?

- Have you experienced the anticipated consequence before?

- Do others agree with your assessment of probability?

- Does common sense support the likelihood of a negative outcome?

- If not, start focusing on more probable —and more motivating—outcomes.

All growth is a risk. To find the courage to move forward, do not focus on possible outcomes, but rather on those that are most probable.

Quick-Lift 87

BUILD YOUR CHANGE MUSCLES

While some opportunities require that you simply jump in with both feet, you can build future flexibility by developing your "change muscles" with small daily risks. As in weight training, once you strengthen your muscles with repetition at one level, you can move to bigger weights.

- Stop right now and strike up a conversation with someone new. Introduce yourself at a coffee shop, bookstore, or fitness center. Or pick up the phone and introduce yourself to a networking prospect.

- If you usually hold back at meetings, speak up first—just for today.

- At lunch, try a new food or eat in a new place.

- Volunteer for a leadership position—chair a committee, run a fundraiser, or spearhead a neighborhood initiative.

- Let down your guard for the next fifteen minutes: apologize for an insensitive remark, admit responsibility for a mistake, or correct a half-truth you inadvertently told.

Don't wait for a big leap to test your courage. Give it a small workout every day. Savor the "kick" you get from stepping out of your comfort zone to connect with a piece of the great unknown.

Quick-Lift 88
CREATE A COURAGE TIMELINE

Every time you take a risk and survive, you strengthen your ability to move forward. However, most of us recall our failures far more vividly than our successes. It's the old nine-one rule. We can receive nine compliments and one criticism in a week and focus on the one criticism. Reverse that rule and you'll be on your way —moving your life forward—no matter what it takes.

- Draw a straight line across the center of a sheet of paper. Using vertical hash marks divide the line into five sections.

- Beginning on the far right, enter the current year under the line at the first hash mark. Moving right to left, enter each year before.

- Now above each section (beginning with this year) list five to six risks you took—as small as speaking up at a meeting for the first time to as large as ending a bad relationship.

- Moving back in time, list risks for each year. How many were a bit rough? How many actually worked out well? How many of them did you survive?

Learn from your mistakes, but focus on your successes. It is there that you will find the courage to try again.

149

Quick-Lift 89
LEAN ON YOUR TEAM

When facing a challenge, it always helps to have a few folks in your corner. People who know you, care about you, and have a vested interest in your success can really give you the push you need when you're hesitating.

- List three people who really believe in you and want to see you succeed.

- Who among them is the best listener—someone who will really hear your concerns?

- Who is a great idea person—ready to help you brainstorm possible strategies?

- Who is the best cheerleader—likely to reinforce your strengths?

- What are you waiting for? Send an S.O.S. right now.

Find a team to serve as your safety net and you'll find your courage building up.

Quick-Lift 90
LET OTHERS INSPIRE YOU

When *our courage is lagging a bit, the strength of others can be most inspiring. They remind us that we are not alone facing a challenge—others face similar or more daunting challenges. Role models also provide perspective. "If they can bravely step forward and cope with the fear," we think, "then surely I can muster the strength I need."*

- **What stories of courage are in today's news?**

- **Which famous people do you admire for their great courage in the face of adversity?** For example, Christopher Reeve and Michael J. Fox have inspired many of us.

- **What children have you heard about, displaying courage greater than their years?** I am reminded of Ryan McCrary, a thirteen-year-old from Oregon, who, battling leukemia and the accompanying trauma of chemotherapy, bravely led a team in a fundraising march for his disease, became a spokesperson for the Make-A-Wish Foundation, and selflessly "coached" younger patients on how to cope with the challenges of the disease.

When we see others cope with their challenges, our own seem more manageable. Courage in any form gives us all hope.

Chapter 10

JUST MY LUCK!

ACKNOWLEDGING
ABUNDANCE

Chapter 10
JUST MY LUCK!

Ever have days when you find yourself focusing on how hard your life is, how unlucky you are, and how unfair it all seems? I'm not talking about major life challenges (illness, divorce, loss of a job), but rather the everyday life-bump stuff (family troubles, money worries, a disgruntled boss). We all can get caught up in poor-me mind chatter from time to time, but it doesn't do us much good. Knee-deep in pity, we feel burdened, weighed down, and stuck in a rut of misfortune. Feeling depleted and helpless, it's hard to muster enthusiasm for anything. "Why bother?" might be your mantra. "It's hopeless. I guess this is just my lot in life." To move from self-pity to joy and optimism takes a shift in focus from what's wrong to what's right. Start acknowledging what you *do* have, instead of focusing on what's missing. What you focus on grows in your life. What you ignore tends to wither away.

Direct your energy toward abundance by acknowledging it, being grateful for it, and sharing it with others. Remove energy from what's wrong by not thinking about it, complaining about it, or resisting it.

This simple shift of attention starts an upward energy spiral. As you notice what's right (a friend's kindness, perhaps), instead of what's wrong (everyone else forgot your birthday), you feel more supported and cared for. When you feel grateful, you are more willing to share your bounty with others. When you give, the flow of abundance returns to you. So, instead of waiting for fate to deal you a better hand, use gratitude to move your life forward.

Abundant living is the fine art of enjoying what you have, sharing what is yours, and attracting what is right.

—Suzanne Zoglio

ELEVEN WAYS TO ACKNOWLEDGE ABUNDANCE!

Whether you've had a streak of bad luck or have just been feeling ignored, these quick-lifts will help you to feel rich from the inside out. When it seems the well is running dry, try one of these ideas to lift yourself up. Read over all ten and then pick one that appeals to you.

91 **Inventory Your Riches**

92 **Accept Free Gifts**

93 **Acknowledge Generosity**

94 **Proclaim Your Love of Life**

95 **Give Thanks for a Glass Half-Full**

96 **Watch for Miracles**

97 **Share Your Bounty**

98 **Go on a Life-Is-Great Date**

99 **Shake Your Bootie**

100 **Stop Asking, "Why Me?"**

101 **Do One Thing You Love Each Day**

Quick-Lift 91
INVENTORY YOUR RICHES

W*hen money is in short supply, our status is compromised, or we've lost an important relationship, we tend to lose track of the gifts that are left. Focusing on what we've lost, or on what we've never had, we pass right by a storehouse of riches.*

- On an index card or paper, make a gratitude list. Across the top, write "Things I'm Grateful For...." Write down everything that comes to mind in the next five minutes, or just keep writing until your pen stops. Among other things, you might consider: material things, physical traits, your intelligence, special talents, personality traits, learning opportunities, relationships, lucky breaks, your heritage, faith, good health, emotional well-being, your career, or livelihood.

Taking stock of all that you have can make you feel "rich" in minutes.

Quick-Lift 92
ACCEPT FREE GIFTS

No matter how poor or deprived you feel, it is difficult to stick with that feeling for very long if you turn your focus to Mother Nature. No high-priced ticket is needed. No fancy clothes are required. You don't even have to be on an in-crowd list. You just have to show up.

- If you're up early today, stop to watch the sunrise.

- On your walk from the bus stop, parking lot, or subway station listen and watch for any birds. Notice their shape, color, song, and habits. See if you can later describe and identify each.

- If you are out on an errand, stop for a minute and appreciate the leaves, shrubs, or a magnificent city skyline.

- If you notice squirrels playing outside of your window, give in and watch "the show" for a few minutes.

The universe provides many wonders; all we have to do is open our eyes.

Quick-Lift 93
ACKNOWLEDGE GENEROSITY

When we do not receive what we wish or expect from those close to us, it is easy to dismiss an intended kindness. If it's not exactly what we were looking for, we might brush off the gesture, depriving ourselves of a gift.

- Try recalling all the kindnesses that have come into your life in the past few weeks. Perhaps someone remembered your birthday, or wished you well on a project, or inquired about your health? Maybe a colleague invited you to lunch or brought you a cup of coffee. Did any one pinch-hit for you, taking something off your plate? Did a friend call to trust you with a secret or share a joyful experience? Were you surprised by a compliment or words of admiration? Maybe someone shared information or made a referral to you? Write down any kindnesses that come to mind.

- If you have not yet done so, stop now to acknowledge each "gift."

Focus on what's missing and life seems bare. Focus on what you've been given, and a rich, full life appears.

160

Quick-Lift 94
PROCLAIM YOUR LOVE OF LIFE

*t is often easier to articulate what we **don't like** about our lives than what we **do like** But, before you can find more of what you want in life, you've got to know what that is.*

- With a heart full of gratitude, silently recount all of the things that you love about your life. Or, if you wish, jot them down so you can review your list at another time. You might start your list off by completing this unfinished sentence: "I really love _____."

- Now, in the next few minutes, express what else you'd really like to come into your life. Think in specifics, creating a detailed picture in your mind.

- You might write down your desires, so you can remember what you'd really love to see in your life.

There is an expression in Alice's Adventures in Wonderland that reads, "If you don't know where you're going, you'll probably end up somewhere else." A corollary might be, "If you don't know what you want in life, you'll probably get something else."

Quick-Lift 95
GIVE THANKS FOR A GLASS HALF-FULL

If life's challenges are taking their toll, you may be focusing on the "hole," instead of the donut. Focusing on what's NOT there keeps us feeling downtrodden. To shift to feeling lucky, acknowledge whatever is going right with your life.

- What do you have to be thankful for today?

- Who are you glad is in your life?

- What "luck" has come your way recently?

You must recognize good fortune before you can feel fortunate.

Quick-Lift 96

WATCH FOR MIRACLES

Feeling down, we often forget to look up. Then the more we ignore wonders large and small, the lower we feel. And yet, it is nearly impossible to catch a glimpse of a newborn child, a goldfinch feeding on thistle, or a bright red sun in the sky and not feel part of something magnificent.

- What miracles of nature have you witnessed already today? A sunrise, a bird in flight, or leaves turning crimson?

- What miracles of the heart have you observed? Someone forgiving you, a helping hand from a friend, or kindness from a stranger?

- What miracles of health have you seen recently? A spontaneous remission of a disease, a speedy recovery after an injury, or a new-found strength?

What "miracle" would you like to see next in your life? Believe it. Watch for it.

Quick-Lift 97
SHARE YOUR BOUNTY

No matter how little you have in the way of material things, you always have inner bounty to share. You have encouraging words, creative ideas, a sense of humor, and the power of prayer. So, even when you feel your luck is running thin, give something away from your bounty within.

- Share a funny story with someone who could use a little cheer.

- Silently say a prayer for someone who is facing a challenge

- Drop a line or call a friend to share an inspiring quote or passage.

- If you get a great idea about someone else's project, share it.

You cannot give what you do not have, so sharing from within reminds you of what you possess.

Quick-Lift 98
GO ON A LIFE-IS-GREAT DATE

W_hen life feels like all work and no play, it's time to celebrate. You don't need a special occasion; it's special enough that it's a new day, you are alive, and the sun is still in the sky._

- When everything's going your way, how do you like to celebrate? Meet a friend, go to a special restaurant, break out the champagne, or indulge in a special edible treat?

- Stop now, and hold a life-is-great ritual.

- Or, if the celebration requires planning, stop now and make the arrangements (invite the people, reserve the table, order the treat, etc.)

- Minimally, write "Life Is Great" on a Post-It Note and place it where you'll see it several times today.

Feeling down, we find no reason to celebrate, yet getting up each day should be reason enough!

Quick-Lift 99
SHAKE YOUR BOOTIE

When *life feels like a grind, change the rhythm. Put on some toe-tapping music and get movin.' Hum, whistle along, or sing out loud. It's difficult to stay down when the joy of music surrounds you.*

- Turn up the radio, pop in a CD, or just hum a favorite tune.

- All alone, behind closed doors, let your happy feet soar. Grab a partner, if you wish (an infant, pet, friend, or coworker) to spread the joy. Kick off your shoes and shake your bootie for one full tune.

- Snap your fingers; jump and shout; knock yourself out.

Whatever your mood, sing, dance, hum, or whistle. Before you know it, others will be commenting on your upbeat attitude.

Quick-Lift 100
STOP ASKING, "WHY ME?"

When *Lady Luck seems to have taken a vacation, and one thing after another goes wrong, you may be tempted to repeatedly ask, "Why me?" Unfortunately, staying with that question too long will keep you stuck right where you are. Instead, accept what is and move on.*

- Consider one recent disappointment or upset. Is there anything you learned from it?

- Given that bad things happen to good people, accept that this isn't your fault or anyone else's. It just is.

- Are you ready to accept this challenge and do whatever you can to move on? If so, what can you do right now to minimize any damage and begin your rebound?

When life doesn't go according to your plans, consider that the alternate path just might lead to something even better.

Quick-Lift 101
DO ONE THING YOU LOVE EACH DAY

For *ongoing optimal energy, invest in something you love every day. Even a few minutes of pure bliss can keep you uplifted. Let's face it, you'll never* **find** *the time to do as you wish; you have to make the time—maybe in little chunks.*

- Think of one interest that you keep "meaning" to explore a bit more—sports cars, flying, tennis, art, opera, boating, woodworking, writing, jazz, advising, mentoring, babysitting. Whatever the interests, they should be things that totally engage you and make you feel more alive when you do them.

- Now, decide on one small thing you can do right now—in ten minutes or less—related to that interest—call someone, check out a related Internet site, order a book, read an article, plan a weekend event, reserve tickets to an expo, sign up for a course, organize related material.

Don't put your passions on hold until you have more time; enjoy them in little bites every day!

"OUT OF CLUTTER, FIND SIMPLICITY. FROM DISCORD FIND HARMONY. IN THE MIDDLE OF DIFFICULTY LIES OPPORTUNITY."

—*Albert Einstein*

ACKNOWLEDGMENTS

I am grateful to many people for facilitating the birth of this book, including many experts in the human potential field who have informed my work with their research, writings, and teachings, especially: Herbert Benson, Jack Canfield, Deepak Chopra, Daniel Goleman, Ken Blanchard, Marjorie Blanchard, Wayne Dyer, and Tara-Bennett Goleman.

It is said that we all stand on the shoulders of many when we succeed. Indeed, it is the brainstorming, feedback, dialogue, and constructive criticism of friends and colleagues that charges me up or calms me down as needed. Thank you to all who shared their thoughts at various stages of this project, especially: Jim Donovan, Elizabeth Doviak, Alan and Susan Elko, Dan Lambert, Bill Lawton, Louis Manzi, Stephanie Marston, Steven Rossi, Michael Stumpf, Rea Boylan Thomas, J. Henry Warren, and Kenneth White.

Sincere appreciation to my copy editor, Alice Lawler, who possesses not only a keen eye and a way with words, but also the warmest of hearts and a most generous spirit.

Heartfelt thanks to my sister Ann and my brothers David and Doug, for being the absolute best ambassadors for my work and loving supporters in all areas of my life.

Finally, it is with love and gratitude that I acknowledge my husband Mike, who has taught me much about publishing, but even more about myself.

SUGGESTED READINGS

Benson, Herbert and Proctor, William. *The Breakout Principle*. New York, NY: Scribner, 2003.

Benson, Herbert and Klipper, Miriam. *The Relaxation Response*. New York, NY: Avon, 1990.

Benson, Herbert with Stark, Marg. *Timeless Healing: The Power and Biology of Belief*. New York, NY: Scribner, 1996.

Bennett-Goleman, Tara. *Emotional Alchemy*. New York, NY: Harmony Books, 2001.

Blanchard, Kenneth and Blanchard, Marjorie. *The One-Minute Manager Balances Work and Life*. New York, NY: William Morrow & Co., 1999.

Blanchard, Kenneth and Sheldon Bowles. *Gung Ho!* New York, NY: William Morrow, 1997.

Canfield, Jack. *Self-Esteem and Peak Performance*. Audio. Career Track Pub.,1995.

Chopra, Deepak. *Ageless Body, Timeless Mind*. New York, NY: Harmony Books, 1993.

_____. *The Seven Spiritual Laws of Success*. San Rafael, CA: Ambler-Allen, 1994.

Dyer, Wayne. *10 Secrets to Success and Inner Peace*. Carlsbad, CA: Hay House, Inc., 2002.

_____. *There's a Spiritual Solution to Every Problem*. New York, NY: HarperCollins, 2001.

Gawain, Shakti. *Creative Visualization*. San Rafael, CA: New World Library, 2002.

Goleman, Daniel. *Emotional Intelligence.* New York, NY: Bantam Books, 1995.

_____. *Destructive Emotions.* New York, NY: Bantam Dell, 2003.

Jeffers, Susan. *Feel the Fear and Do It Anyway.* New York, NY: Fawcett Columbine, 1987.

Johnson, Spencer and Blanchard, Kenneth. *Who Moved My Cheese?* New York, NY: Putnam, 1998.

Seligman, Martin. *Authentic Happiness.* New York, NY: The Free Press, 2002.

Williamson, Marianne. *Everyday Grace.* New York, NY: Riverhead Books, 2002.

Young, J.E. and Klosko, J.S. *Reinventing Your Life.* New York, NY: Penguin Books, 1994.

Zoglio, Suzanne. *Create a Life That Tickles Your Soul.* Doylestown, PA: Tower Hill Press, 2000.

INDEX

ABOUT THE AUTHOR

SUZANNE ZOGLIO is often described as "a master energizer." For over twenty years she has coached executives, facilitated team-building meetings, and presented self-development seminars to audiences in the US and Europe. Her corporate clients include small businesses, government agencies, and Fortune 500 companies including American Express, Hewlett-Packard, Lockheed Martin, and GlaxoSmithKline.

Suzanne has appeared on radio and television in more than twenty-five states, has been published in over thirty business journals in the United States, Singapore, Canada, and England, and has been featured as a life-balance expert in such popular magazines as *Cosmopolitan, First for Women, Marie-Claire, Fitness Magazine,* and *Prevention.*

A native of Rhode Island, Suzanne moved to Bucks County, PA in 1972. She holds a master's degree in counseling and a doctorate in organizational psychology.

Listen to audio of Dr. Sue or preview a demo videotape on her website at *www.zoglio.com* where you also can subscribe to her FREE motivational newsletter, read book excerpts, and download motivational articles.

OTHER BOOKS BY SUZANNE ZOGLIO

Create a Life That Tickles Your Soul (Tower Hill Press, 2000)
Named "Outstanding Book of the Year–Most Life-Changing" in the Independent Publisher Book Awards 2000.

Teams At Work: 7 Keys To Success (Tower Hill Press, 1997)

Training Program for Teams At Work (Tower Hill Press, 1997)

The Participative Leader (McGraw-Hill, 1994)

All books are available at bookstores nationwide,
from all online booksellers, at *www.zoglio.com,*
or by calling 1-888-307-8807.